Psychoanalytic Perspecti
Fundamentalism, Radic
and Terrorism

Terrorism is no longer woven into the backdrop of our daily lives, but rather it has been pushed to centre stage – an ongoing tragedy in which comprehension of the perpetrators' motivations is eclipsed by the impact of horror and devastation on its victims and wider society. Attempting to make sense of these atrocities and their antecedents, a body of literature has accumulated since 9/11 which offers a psychoanalytic perspective on terrorism. This research provides a reflective space within which the unconscious motivations, primitive conflicts, fantasies and impulses that underpin the extreme mindsets and violent actions of the individuals and groups involved may be explored, offering insights complementary to those of different disciplines – sociological, political, cultural and other.

This book brings together contemporary psychoanalytic writers and practitioners involved in the study of radicalisation, fundamentalism and terrorism. Some of the authors have worked with terrorists, thus grounding their reflections and insights in direct clinical contact with these individuals. Understanding the motivations of the perpetrators includes elucidation of the wider group dynamics of minority populations, where the perpetuation of violence that is seen as terrorism may be viewed by its perpetrators as a justifiable response to collective experiences of subjugation, humiliation and injustice suffered over generations. Understanding such perspectives is not colluding with the aggressors, but rather it may contribute to interventions at both individual and global levels that attempt to break the deadly cycle of violence.

This book was originally published as two special issues of *Psychoanalytic Psychotherapy*.

Jessica Yakeley is a Consultant Psychiatrist in Forensic Psychotherapy at the Portman Clinic, London, UK and Director of Medical Education and Associate Medical Director of the Tavistock and Portman NHS Foundation Trust, London, UK. She is a Fellow of the British Psychoanalytic Society, London, UK and Editor of *Psychoanalytic Psychotherapy*.

Paul Cundy is a Consultant Adult Psychotherapist and a Psychodynamic Psychotherapy Lead at North East London NHS Foundation Trust, UK. He is an Associate Fellow of the British Psychological Society, Leicester, UK and Assistant Editor of *Psychoanalytic Psychotherapy*.

Psychoanalytic Perspectives on Fundamentalism, Radicalisation and Terrorism

Edited by
Jessica Yakeley and Paul Cundy

Routledge
Taylor & Francis Group
LONDON AND NEW YORK

First published 2019
by Routledge
2 Park Square, Milton Park, Abingdon, Oxon, OX14 4RN, UK

and by Routledge
52 Vanderbilt Avenue, New York, NY 10017, USA

First issued in paperback 2020

Routledge is an imprint of the Taylor & Francis Group, an informa business

British Library Cataloguing-in-Publication Data
A catalogue record for this book is available from the British Library

ISBN 13: 978-0-367-58239-5 (pbk)
ISBN 13: 978-0-367-03039-1 (hbk)

Typeset in Times New Roman
by codeMantra

Publisher's Note
The publisher accepts responsibility for any inconsistencies that may have arisen during the conversion of this book from journal articles to book chapters, namely the possible inclusion of journal terminology.

Contents

Citation Information vii

Notes on Contributors ix

Introduction 1
Jessica Yakeley

1 One man's freedom fighter is another man's terrorist: a selected overview of the psychoanalytic and group analytic study of terrorism 6
Pamela Kleinot

2 Fundamentalism, Radicalization and Terrorism. Part 1: terrorism as dissolution in a complex system 19
John, Lord Alderdice

3 Fundamentalism, Radicalization and Terrorism. Part 2: fundamentalism, regression and repair 35
John, Lord Alderdice

4 Inflammatory projective identification in fundamentalist religious and economic terrorism 48
David Morgan

5 Rage and hatred in infants: conditions which facilitate development versus those which result in tragic delays or alarming distortions 61
Anne Alvarez

6 Terror, fundamentalism, and male adolescence 70
Elisabeth Rohr

7 Dreaming of Columbine: exploring an offender's preoccupation with the Columbine Massacre 82
Maktuno Suit

8 Pathways into terrorism: the Good, the Bad and the Ugly 94
Monica Lloyd and Pamela Kleinot

9 Terrorism and mental disorder, and the role of psychiatrists in counter-terrorism in the UK 105
Jessica Yakeley and Richard Taylor

10 Working together to break the 'circles of fear' between Muslim communities and mental health services 120
Angela Byrne, Shirin Mustafa and Imam Qamruzzaman Miah

11 The challenge of radicalisation: a public health approach to understanding and intervention 128
Kamaldeep Bhui and Edgar Jones

Index 139

Citation Information

The chapters in this book were originally published in *Psychoanalytic Psychotherapy*, volume 31, issue 3 (September 2017) and issue 4 (December 2017). When citing this material, please use the original page numbering for each article, as follows:

Introduction
Jessica Yakeley
Psychoanalytic Psychotherapy, volume 31, issue 3 (September 2017) pp. 267–271

Chapter 1
One man's freedom fighter is another man's terrorist: a selected overview of the psychoanalytic and group analytic study of terrorism
Pamela Kleinot
Psychoanalytic Psychotherapy, volume 31, issue 3 (September 2017) pp. 272–284

Chapter 2
Fundamentalism, Radicalization and Terrorism. Part 1: terrorism as dissolution in a complex system
John, Lord Alderdice
Psychoanalytic Psychotherapy, volume 31, issue 3 (September 2017) pp. 285–300

Chapter 3
Fundamentalism, Radicalization and Terrorism. Part 2: fundamentalism, regression and repair
John, Lord Alderdice
Psychoanalytic Psychotherapy, volume 31, issue 3 (September 2017) pp. 301–313

Chapter 4
Inflammatory projective identification in fundamentalist religious and economic terrorism
David Morgan
Psychoanalytic Psychotherapy, volume 31, issue 3 (September 2017) pp. 314–326

Chapter 5

Rage and hatred in infants: conditions which facilitate development versus those which result in tragic delays or alarming distortions
Anne Alvarez
Psychoanalytic Psychotherapy, volume 31, issue 3 (September 2017) pp. 327–335

Chapter 6

Terror, fundamentalism, and male adolescence
Elisabeth Rohr
Psychoanalytic Psychotherapy, volume 31, issue 4 (December 2017) pp. 343–354

Chapter 7

Dreaming of Columbine: exploring an offender's preoccupation with the Columbine Massacre
Maktuno Suit
Psychoanalytic Psychotherapy, volume 31, issue 4 (December 2017) pp. 355–366

Chapter 8

Pathways into terrorism: the Good, the Bad and the Ugly
Monica Lloyd and Pamela Kleinot
Psychoanalytic Psychotherapy, volume 31, issue 4 (December 2017) pp. 367–377

Chapter 9

Terrorism and mental disorder, and the role of psychiatrists in counter-terrorism in the UK
Jessica Yakeley and Richard Taylor
Psychoanalytic Psychotherapy, volume 31, issue 4 (December 2017) pp. 378–392

Chapter 10

Working together to break the 'circles of fear' between Muslim communities and mental health services
Angela Byrne, Shirin Mustafa and Imam Qamruzzaman Miah
Psychoanalytic Psychotherapy, volume 31, issue 4 (December 2017) pp. 393–400

Chapter 11

The challenge of radicalisation: a public health approach to understanding and intervention
Kamaldeep Bhui and Edgar Jones
Psychoanalytic Psychotherapy, volume 31, issue 4 (December 2017) pp. 401–410

Notes on Contributors

John, Lord Alderdice's areas of special interest are the individual and group psychology of terrorism and violent political conflict, the psychology of religious fundamentalism and the study of relations between groups of indigenous people and settler communities. He remains directly involved in analyses and interventions in political conflicts in various parts of the world and is the Director of the Centre for the Resolution of Intractable Conflict at Harris Manchester College, University of Oxford and a Clinical Professor in Psychiatry at the University of Maryland in Baltimore, USA.

Anne Alvarez is a consultant child and adolescent psychotherapist and retired co-chair of the Autism Service, Tavistock Clinic, London. She was Visiting Professor at the San Francisco Psychoanalytic Society and Institute, USA in November 2005 and is an Honorary Member of the Psychoanalytic Centre of California, Los Angeles, USA. Her research interests include the psychoanalysis of babies, psychotherapeutic intervention and paedopsychological trauma.

Kamaldeep Bhui, Professor is a clinical academic psychiatrist and psychoanalytic psychotherapist. He is Head of Centre for Psychiatry, Barts and The London School of Medicine & Dentistry, at QMUL and editor of British Journal of Psychiatry, and College Editor chairing the publications management board of the Royal College of Psychiatrists. He is Director of the Synergi Collaborative Centre on ethnic inequalities, severe mental illness and multiple disadvantage (www.synergicollaborativecentre.co.uk); Director of the Cultural Consultation Service at QMUL (www.Culturalconsultion.org) and Director of MSc Creative Arts & Mental Health.

Angela Byrne is a Clinical Psychologist at the East London NHS Foundation Trust, UK. She obtained a professional doctorate from the University of East London, UK and was awarded her PhD in Psychology from Royal Holloway, University of London, UK. Her clinical and research interests include improving service provision for marginalised communities, narrative therapy and community psychology.

Edgar Jones is the Programme Leader for the MSc in War and Psychiatry at the Institute of Psychiatry, Psychology & Neuroscience, King's College London, UK. His research focuses on how soldiers and civilians cope with the stress of war and investigates its impact on their psychological health in the aftermath of conflict. He also investigates vulnerability to radicalisation, whilst the psychological dimension of terrorism is an ongoing research focus.

Pamela Kleinot is a psychotherapist, group analyst, conference organiser and documentary film-maker. Her research interests include the 'war on terror', psychoanalytical approaches to the unconscious roots of aggression, hatred and violence and using group analysis to understand social processes as people are social beings.

Monica Lloyd is a forensic psychologist who gained her professional qualifications within the Prison Service and over the course of her career worked both in prisons and in HM Inspectorate of Prisons where her interest in extremism was kindled from the inspection of the Maze prison in Northern Ireland. Her later work developing a methodology for assessing risk and needs in extremist offenders for the National Offender Management Service (now HMPPS) has become a common assessment framework across the criminal justice system in England and Wales. She continues to work in the area of counter-terrorism, and part-time as Senior Lecturer in the Centre for Applied Psychology at the University of Birmingham.

Imam Qamruzzaman Miah is a Mental Health Practitioner and an Imam at the Department of Spiritual, Religious and Cultural Care of East London NHS Foundation Trust. His work aims to promote understanding of mental health, religion and spirituality and build bridges between Mental Health Services and Muslim communities.

David Morgan is a psychoanalyst and consultant psychotherapist who worked for many years at the Portman Clinic, London, UK and later as a specialist consultant with migrants, asylum seekers and political groups, and in full time private practice. He is co-editor with Stan Ruszczynski of *Violence Perversion and Delinquency* (2014) and *The Political Mind* (in Press). He is chair of The Political Mind Seminars at the British Psychoanalytic Society and a member of International Psychoanalytic Associations Committee for Humanitarian Organisations. He lecturers nationally and internationally and was organiser of the Frontier Psychoanalyst broadcasts and podcast.

Shirin Mustafa is completing her professional doctorate in clinical psychology at the University of Hertfordshire. Her publications and research interests include working with Black and minority ethnic communities and faith groups as well as religion, spirituality and mental health.

Elisabeth Rohr was Professor for Intercultural Education at the Philipps University, Marburg/Germany till 2013. As a group analyst, coach and trainer she has been working in national and international, profit and non-profit organizations. She has established a group analytic supervision training in Guatemala for human rights activists, offered workshops in Palestine for psychologists and has been an external examiner for the Irish Group Analytic Institute.

Currently she is engaged as a supervisor in Denmark and has been involved in organizing a summer school about "Memory and Migration" in Colombia. Her research interests include migration, fundamentalism, female and male adolescence and intercultural supervision. She has published extensively about these topics.

Maktuno Suit is an Independent Researcher and a Psychotherapist and Organisational Consultant. His research interests include radicalisation, extremism, the Columbine Massacre, jihadism and personality disorders. He was previously a Group Psychotherapist for the Ministry of Justice, City of Westminster, UK and a Psychodynamic Psychotherapist for Newham Secondary Care Psychological Services, London, UK.

Richard Taylor is a consultant forensic psychiatrist at the North London Forensic Service. His clinical work includes the Fixated Threat Assessment Centre and the Counter Terror Liaison and Diversion Team. He is a member of the Strategic Management Board for MAPPA in London. His areas of interest and expertise include: psychiatric assessment of serious and violent offending, terrorism, fixated threat assessment, fraud and malingering, prison mental health, medical ethics and MAPPA.

Jessica Yakeley is a consultant psychiatrist in forensic psychotherapy and Director of the Portman Clinic, and Director of Medical Education, Tavistock and Portman NHS Foundation Trust. She is also a fellow of the British Psychoanalytic Society and editor of the journal Psychoanalytic Psychotherapy. Her particular fields of interest and research include antisocial personality disorder, violence, paraphilias, risk, and psychodynamic methods of teaching about the doctor patient relationship. She is the author of *Working with Violence: A Contemporary Psychoanalytic Approach* (Palgrave MacMillan (2010), and has edited four other books. She is currently Vice Chair of the Royal College of Psychiatrists Psychotherapy Faculty and Research Lead for the British Psychoanalytic Council.

Introduction

Jessica Yakeley

Thinking about radicalisation, fundamentalism and terrorism immediately evokes powerful emotional responses and pushes us to the limits of our sympathy and understanding. Caught up in a maelstrom of public outrage, hate, fear, grief and helplessness is it possible to think psychotherapeutically, to access compassionate feelings and understanding for the perpetrators as well as the victims, to put into words what are often referred to as 'unspeakable' atrocities, and to imagine the mind of the terrorist, rather than adopting an overview and global analysis of the subject to distance oneself from any personal encounter?

A popular and plausible understanding of the nature and relationship between fundamentalism, radicalisation and terrorism is as follows. The first expresses a belief system of extreme views, usually pertaining to religion, in upholding a strict, literal or distorted interpretation of scripture, but also includes strict adherence to the basic principles of any subject or discipline. The second describes the process by which an individual, or group comes to adopt these (usually) extreme religious views which have now become attached to political or social ideals and aspirations that reject or undermine the status quo or contemporary ideas often associated with Western values. This process is often thought to be the result of the active work of fundamentalists in causing someone, thought to be young and vulnerable in some way to being 'converted', to adopt radical positions on religious, political or social issues. Finally, in the most extreme cases, a minority of the radicalised will turn to terrorism in the unlawful use of violence and intimidation in the pursuit of political aims. From a psychoanalytic viewpoint, radicalisation, fundamentalism and terrorism all involve disturbed states of mind and it is tempting to understand the relationship between the three as a pathological regression of psychic processes from the psychic, to psychotic thinking, to violent enactment, where highly disturbing thoughts, fantasies and affective states are expelled in action. However, as John, Lord Alderdice points out in this issue, although radicalisation, fundamentalism and terrorism tend to become fused in the public mind, there is not a simple linear relationship between the three phenomena, nor can one assume that all result from pathological processes.

The idea for this Special Issue, published in two consecutive issues, was first suggested to me at the end of 2015 by Pam Kleinot, who was organising two conferences on the subject: 'Radicalisation, fundamentalism, gangs and vulnerability' and 'Radicalisation, terrorism and hate', both of which took place very successfully at Amnesty International, Human Rights Action Centre in London last year. At that time, the international community was reeling from the deadliest terrorist attack in French history, in which ISIS claimed responsibility for multiple shootings, hostage taking and bombing in Paris in November 2015, which left 130 people dead and 368 injured. This attack, of course, had occurred after another terrorist attack in Paris earlier that year, which killed 17 and injured 22, in which the antifascist satirical magazine, Charlie Hebdo, was the target of a mass shooting by two Islamic gunmen who identified themselves as belonging to Al-Qaeda.

At the time of submitting the first draft of their paper 'The challenge of radicalisation: a public health approach to understanding and intervention', Kham Bhui and Edgar Jones wrote that since 7/7 there had been only been eight deaths as a result of terrorism within the UK: Mohammed Saleem, a 82-year-old Muslim stabbed by Pavlo Lapshyn, a 25-year-old Ukrainian student in April 2013; Private Lee Rigby stabbed in May 2013, by Michael Adebolajo and Michael Adebowale near the Royal Artillery Barracks in Woolwich; Jo Cox, killed by Thomas Mair in June 2016; and the five who died on Westminster Bridge in March 2017. However, during the process of editing their paper, this figure had to be increased five-fold to an overall total of 39 people killed in the UK since 2005, following the spate of terrorist attacks: 22 killed by a suicide bomber in Manchester, eight killed in the London Bridge attack and one person in an attack at a mosque in Finsbury Park in June 2017. Terrorism is no longer woven into the backdrop of our daily lives: it has been pushed centre stage into an on-going tragedy from which few can avoid being affected.

In the wake of 9/11 and the rise of suicide bombers in the Middle Eastern conflict, a body of literature has accumulated offering a psychoanalytic perspective on terrorism. Psychoanalysis, of course, is only one discipline of many that attempts to make sense of these events and the motivations of those responsible, and offers insights that are complementary to other approaches – sociological, political, cultural and others. This Special Issue brings together contemporary psychoanalytic writers and practitioners, some of whom were speakers at the aforementioned conferences, involved in the study of radicalisation, fundamentalism and terrorism. Some of the authors have worked with terrorists, thus, grounding their reflections and insights in direct clinical contact with these individuals. Although the contributors to this volume approach these subjects from different angles, all are united in acknowledging the importance of unconscious primitive psychic mechanisms – phantasies, conflicts and defences – that may underlie the extreme mindsets and violent actions of the individuals and groups involved.

Pam Kleinot starts off the first issue with an informed overview of the psychoanalytic and group analytic study of terrorism in her paper 'One man's freedom fighter is another man's terrorist' which tries to make sense of the unconscious roots of aggression, hatred and violence. She reminds us that terrorism is often a social activity and therefore, a group analytic approach has an important contribution to make in understanding the unconscious dynamics of large groups that play a crucial role in the development of radicalisation, fundamentalism and terrorism.

This group perspective is reinforced by the subsequent two papers by John, Lord Alderdice: 'Fundamentalism, radicalisation and terrorism Part 1: Terrorism as dissolution in a complex system' and 'Fundamentalism, radicalisation and terrorism Part 2: Fundamentalism, regression and repair'. Drawing on his personal experience of growing up in Northern Ireland, and his unique position as both a prominent politician and psychoanalytic psychiatrist working with terrorist organisations in countries involved in political conflicts around the world, he provides a psychoanalytic and systemic perspective on the history of fundamentalism, radicalisation and terrorism and explores how the group dynamics of minority populations may result in the perpetuation of violence that is seen as terrorism by others, but for whom it is a justifiable response to collective experiences of subjugation, humiliation and injustice suffered over generations.

Expanding on Alderdice's ideas with Kleinian theory, David Morgan, in his powerfully evocative paper 'Inflammatory projective identification in fundamentalist religious and economic terrorism', sees the rise of fundamentalism and terrorism as a retreat from the anxieties provoked by a modern world characterised by industrialisation, urbanisation, secularism and technology. He likens the terrorist mindset to a psychotic illness, where we are the unwilling container for explosive attacks, the aim of which is to communicate fragmentation and psychosis into the minds and bodies of the victims, via the process of what Morgan calls 'inflammatory projective identification'.

The next two papers together consider developmental trajectories and risk factors for the onset of violence, radicalisation and fundamentalism in childhood and adolescence. In her paper 'Rage and hatred in infants: Conditions which facilitate development vs. those which result in tragic delays or alarming distortions', Anne Alvarez draws on her extensive experience with violent children who have been abused or neglected, to distinguish, within the context of internal object relationships, three factors contributing to violent behaviour: disturbance, deviance, and deficit and neglect, and links each of these to the child's relationship with the object. In disturbance, aggression may arise towards a persecutory object and where this internalised violence may be turned against the self. Some infants and children may be pushed into a perverse trajectory where they become identified with the bad object, violence becomes a habitual way of relating to others, and they become addicted to perverse excitements. This trajectory has a poor prognosis in being more likely to develop into psychopathy and frank perversion in adulthood. Neglect may be as damaging as frank abuse in producing deficits in the internal representation of good figures and of a good self, which may produce rage, despair and shame, and which eventually harden into deep cynicism and the devaluation of human relationships.

In the following paper, 'Terror, fundamentalism and male adolescence', Elisabeth Rohr examines the next stage of human development – adolescence – and proposes that a male adolescent identity crisis is a risk factor for terrorism in some young men. By linking contemporary theories of religious fundamentalism with psychoanalytic theories of adolescent breakdown, she proposes that boys who have experienced pathological attachments in early childhood, poverty, and difficulties at school and with peers, may be particularly susceptible to being drawn into religious fundamentalist communities which offer containment and a male identity that is fused with a higher being and so has no need for the ambivalence, anxieties and conflicts faced in adolescence.

The second issue describes the work of clinicians who have worked directly with convicted terrorists or those deemed at risk of radicalisation. There is little evidence in the literature of cases of direct therapeutic work with radicalised individuals or terrorists, and therefore, Maktuno Suit's account of her treatment of a young man at risk of radicalisation is unusual. In 'Dreaming of Columbine: Exploring an offender's preoccupation with the Columbine Killings', she describes a compelling clinical case which nicely illustrates Rohr's theory of adolescent vulnerability, fundamentalism and extremism, in her treatment of a young offender, who had converted to Islam in prison and who incited others to join the Taliban and commit suicide bombings. He had experienced in childhood the risk factors that Rohr highlights: poor attachment to his mother, being bullied at school and poor academic achievement, and Maktuno relates how his obsession and identification with the 'Colombine Massacre' killers – two young men who had also experienced bullying and who exacted their revenge in the mass killing of their peers – provided an escape from painful feelings of shame and humiliation. In her psychoanalytically informed treatment of him, paying particular attention to her countertransference, she was able to demonstrate to colleagues the value of a psychoanalytic approach in identifying unconscious factors that contribute to risk assessment, working within a criminal justice system where treatment is focused on cognitive and behavioural modification.

The next two papers reflect the work of clinicians who have worked with convicted terrorists. In 'Pathways into terrorism: The Good, the bad and the ugly', Monica Lloyd and Pam Kleinot put forward a pathway model of terrorism using psychoanalytic and group analytic understanding to reflect on the first author's work with convicted terrorists in prison. By exploring the different motivations of these men, the authors found that they could be divided into three main groups, representing three different pathways into terrorism: those who identified with a noble cause, those who were mainly motivated by criminality, and those, mostly lone actors, who were motivated by hostility and grievance, but who also had higher levels of mental illness than group actors. They propose that for all three groups, terrorism may be understood as a form of communication in which primal fears, existential threats and disavowed feelings are projected via primitive defence mechanisms into a persecuting group which becomes a target for annihilation.

Lloyd and Kleinot's typology of terrorism based on their clinical experience of a small sample of convicted terrorists, is validated by more formal empirical research, which is presented in the paper 'Terrorism and mental disorder, and the role of psychiatrists in counter-terrorism in the UK' by Jessica Yakeley and Richard Taylor, informed by the second author's experience of assessing several incarcerated remand and convicted terrorists. They describe the results of recent studies that have examined the characteristics of the largest sample of terrorists to date, comparing 119 lone actor terrorists with 428 group-based actors, and found that a large proportion of the lone-based actors (41%) had a history of mental health problems and were 13.5 times more likely to have a history of mental illness than group-based terrorists. This contradicts the belief over the past few decades that terrorists were no more likely to suffer from mental disorder than the general population, one explanation being that mental illness would impede decision-making and reliability in executing terrorist acts. Yakeley and Taylor go on to explore the ethical dilemmas encountered by psychiatrists', and other mental health professionals', involvement in the government's strategy to prevent terrorism.

One of the concerns of the government's Prevent strategy and focus on radicalisation is that it has disproportionally targeted Muslims and thus alienated Muslim communities, creating 'circles of fear' in the relationships between these communities and mental health and other services. In their paper 'Working together to break the "circles of fear" between Muslim communities and mental health services', Angela Byrne, Shirin Mustafa and Imam Qamruz Zaman Miah describe their difficult work within Tower Hamlets, East London, with community groups, faith leaders and local services, aimed at breaking these cycles of distrust and animosity, and promoting mutual understanding and respect to improve relationships with mental health services, including better access to talking therapies.

The final paper, 'The challenge of radicalisation: A public health approach to understanding and intervention', echoes the importance of working directly with Muslim communities to understand the meaning of radicalisation and to develop effective interventions at a population level to prevent radicalisation at an early stage of the trajectory of individuals at risk. Kam Bhui and Edgard Jones describe their research in carrying out a large survey of over 600 Pakistani and Bangladeshi men and women living in the community to elucidate risk and protective factors. In contrast to the Prevent strategy, this public health approach focuses on prevention at a population level, seeks to provide evidence-based information to the wider public so that all can see themselves as part of a solution, and reduce the polarisation between those that feel suspect and excluded, and the wider population whose fear and outrage provokes harsh responses, fuelling the 'circles of fear' described in the previous paper. Bhui and Jones' conclusion to their paper eloquently summarises the collective contribution of all of these papers in offering psychoanalytic perspectives on radicalisation, fundamentalism and terrorism: 'The place of psychoanalytic thought lies in not only interrogating the evidence and emotional processes of perpetrators, but also the emotional processes of political decision makers and victims, the media and the wider public'.

One man's freedom fighter is another man's terrorist: a selected overview of the psychoanalytic and group analytic study of terrorism

Pamela Kleinot

This paper is an attempt to understand the significant increase in terrorism worldwide following the 9/11 Al-Quaida bombings which triggered the Bush Administration's "war on terror", leading to two wars and ultimately to the emergence of Daesh. I explore the motivation for social violence as terrorism, which can be carried out by the state or by its citizens, and look at how one man's freedom fighter is another's terrorist. The paper looks at why seemingly ordinary people are converted into 'homegrown' jihadists and how alienation and shame are the driving forces of violence. I give a selected overview of psychoanalytical ideas that try to make sense of the unconscious roots of aggression, hatred and violence. As terrorism is a social activity group analysis has an important contribution to make in understanding the violence of large groupings. The media has a crucial role to play as sensationalist coverage of violence provides terrorists with a free media platform. Both the media and terrorists need an audience and feed off each other. This paper will explore these themes.

> Living in a state of terror was new to many white people in America (after 9/11) ... But black people have been living in a state of terror in this country for more than 400 years – Maya Angelou (Guardian, 2014)
>
> Poverty is the worst form of violence – Mahatma Gandhi

Terrorism has increased significantly worldwide following the Al-Quaida 9/11 bombings in the US in 2001, which triggered the Bush Administration's 'war on terror'. The US and Britain invaded Afghanistan later that year and the UK again joined the US-led invasion of Iraq in 2003. Daesh, commonly known as ISIS, surfaced in 2004. London was hit by the 7/7 bombings in 2005. There has been a wave of terrorist attacks throughout Europe, the US, the Middle East, Africa, Indonesia and other parts of the world ever since.

Terrorism, sometimes described as the poor man's atom bomb, is derived from the Latin word *Terrere* which means to terrify, frighten and startle. The common explanation for the escalation of terrorist incidents is the rise in fundamentalist Islam. Although the emergence of Daesh has been attributed directly to the invasion of Iraq, this development has been fuelled by military interventions in the Middle East coupled with increasing poverty and inequality between rich and poor countries. Billions spent on the wars in the Middle East has not curbed terrorism. In fact, it has led to more violence and intensified an 'us and them mentality' as well as increased polarisation between Muslims and non-Muslims. Daesh uses social media to radicalise, recruit and raise funds. The films of executions and other atrocities are shocking. Most people are disgusted and frightened by the beheadings accompanied by a smiling and proud murderer justifying the action. Yet, others are inspired by these images. The impact is intensified when the perpetrators are revealed as converts to Daesh who have grown up in Western countries.

The word terrorist is used indiscriminately as a synonym for rebel, insurgent, freedom fighter or revolutionary. Are the terms interchangeable? After all, one man's freedom fighter is another's terrorist. Is the motivation for the one the same as for the other? Blackwell (2012) has taken pains to stress that when people are blocked from full access to political institutions, and/or when such institutions are systemically biased against them, terrorism must be seen as a form of legitimate political action. Blackwell refers to Sartre (1961) who says in the preface to Frantz Fanon's *Wretched of the Earth* that when the oppressed resort to violence, it should be recognised that the initial violence is to be found in the system of oppression.

Although terrorist acts can be a means to an end, they can be an end in themselves. Alderdice (2002) distinguishes ordinary crime from terrorism: 'Terrorism is not a belief system but a tactic (involving) the pre-mediated use of violence to create a climate of fear, but is aimed at a wider target than the immediate victims of violence (p. 11).'

The story of Nelson Mandela puts into context that one man's terrorist is another man's freedom fighter. Mandela, who spent 27 years in jail for his terrorist activities, is testimony to how his fight for freedom won the day. He became one of the most venerated world leaders. Of course South Africa was ruled by terror and met with resistance, but ultimately it was through international sanctions and negotiations that the country was able to hold its first democratic multi-racial elections in 1994.

The complexity of terrorist vs freedom fighter is highlighted by De Zulueta (2006) who argues that Osama Bin Laden and 50,000 fighters worldwide were recruited and trained by Pakistan and the US (who also funded the operation, as did the UK and Saudi Arabia).

> These men were feted as 'freedom fighters' in the White House and Downing Street in 1989 (and it may well be that we owe the final collapse of the Soviet Union partly to Bin Laden and his followers). Similarly, the Taliban were trained by Pakistan with the backing of the US and the UK (p. 14).

How are seemingly ordinary people converted into 'homegrown' jihadists? 'Radicalisation' is the term often used to describe the conversion of young people to terrorism, although traditionally the word radical is used in a less pejorative political sense. One factor in their conversion is that many have grown up in the 'war on terror generation' and resent the negative portrayal of Muslims in the barrage of Islamophobia. Horrific images of them are transmitted into smartphones and social media feeds. Another factor is increasing social and economic inequality and racism, which fuels feelings of exclusion, alienation and other grievances.

At this time of heightened global insecurity and fear of terrorism, considerable intellectual and research activity is underway to try to make sense of it all. This involves many fields of study including sociology and social psychology, history, economics and religion. Psychoanalysis has always focused on the causes and consequences of violence and aggression. However, terrorism is a social activity. What goes on in the mind of the terrorist always occurs in a social context. Therefore, group analysis, with its roots in both psychoanalysis and sociology, has an important contribution to make.

How can psychoanalysis and group analysis help us understand this?

Psychoanalysts have argued that unconsciously hate is just as basic to our instinctual make-up as its opposite, love. In *Terrorism and War: Unconscious Dynamics of Political Violence*, Arundale (2002) comments that Freud's (1920) idea of the 'death instinct' was taken further by Klein's hypothesis that it is the source of envy, which requires deflection outwards because it is so threatening (Klein, 1946/1975). This, in turn, makes the individual fearful of attacks by others. However, Arundale notes that this view has been challenged by many psychoanalysts, such as Kohut (1972), who linked the origins of hatred to the universal 'narcisstic wound', and Fairbairn (1952), who held that in the context of relationships frustration fosters hatred.

Several concepts from the work of Freud are helpful in understanding terrorism. These include the repetition compulsion (Freud, 1920) through which a previous situation is re-enacted in an unconscious attempt to master the anxieties associated with it, and annihilation anxiety concerning survival, self-preservation and safety. Using ideas from contemporary psychoanalysis, Meloy and Yakeley (2014) refer to Fonagy's proposition that membership of the large group activates the attachment system, a psychological process which offers the individual a sense of belonging and safety. However, when group participation is troubled, the dynamics of broken and disrupted attachments prevail. Many psychoanalytical ideas about trauma and violence are relevant to the study of terrorism, especially in connection with individual and group identity. Kleinot (2011) has shown that behind every act of violence, there is the pain of trauma, loss, helplessness and rage. De Zulueta (1993) has argued that the cause of violence is 'attachment gone wrong' – that trauma breeds violence breeds trauma breeds violence, especially when traumatised people are unable to narrate their experiences to other people who can understand their communications. Terrorism is potentially a meaningful communication that must be understood in the context of the more general state of mind in which the capacity to think, symbolise and reflect is absent.

Looking at the terrorist-prone individual, Akhtar (2002) quoting Volkan (1997) writes that most major players in a terrorist organisation are, themselves, deeply traumatised individuals. As children they suffered chronic physical abuse and profound emotional humiliation. Quoting Sandler (1987), he argues that the 'safety feeling', necessary for healthy psychic growth, was violated. Trevmow and Sacco (2002, p.107) quote Volkan (1999) that a familiar enemy helps contain and hold disavowed self- and object representations. Akhtar (2002) argues that the terrorist leader appeals to group members' infantile hunger for love and acceptance and offers potential recruits what is in effect a new family, putting himself in the role of the good father. He emphasises that a terrorist-prone individual is pushed over the edge by a trigger from the environment. This may be a new trauma to oneself or family or ethnic group, experienced as an injustice or insult to personal and/or group honour. 'Feeling itself to be a victim, the group begins to victimise others in an act of externalisation (p. 91).'

Volkan (1988) highlights the importance of studying large group identity in shaping the terrorist's core individual identity. He argues that large group identity emerges through shared mental representations of the large group history. These include historical traumas and triumphs involving collective pride and shame. These have been unconsciously chosen and ritualised by the group in the service of group cohesion, helping differentiate the group from the enemy.

The dynamics of large groups foster regression among its members from higher mental functioning to more primitive mental states. To describe the turbulent feelings of a large group under threat, Volkan uses the metaphor of the tent. The canvas of a tent, which is loose-fitting, allows a huge number of individuals to share a sense of sameness with others who are in the same tent. When the tent is perceived to be under threat, group identity is shaken, which often leads to violent revenge for a perceived injustice.

Group analysis helps explain these processes, particularly the endless trans-generational cycle of violence, retaliation and revenge associated with terrorist activities. Foulkes stressed 'man's social nature as basic' (Foulkes, 1964/1984. p. 108). A key tenet of group analysis is that communication is used to keep people talking, not fighting and killing each other. Individuals are nodal points in a communication network. Health is defined in terms of the 'free flow of communication and ill-health in terms of a blockage in it' which Foulkes referred to as an 'autistic symptom … it mumbles to itself secretly, hoping to be overheard' (Foulkes & Anthony, 1957/1984, p. 259). In group analytic terms, a group of 8–15 people is likely to recapitulate the dynamics of the family; 16–32 people to recapitulate groupings such as a classroom; and more than 32 reflects society.

Nitsun's (1991) concept of 'anti-group', which describes the destructive aspect of groups, is helpful in understanding terrorism. He views terrorism as one group projecting its envy, hatred and sadistic fantasies onto another group with the aim of annihilation (personal communication, 2017). In *The Anti-Group* (1996), Nitsun's emphasis on the destructive threat in groups is based on primitive systems of intragroup defence. Reflecting on emotional disturbance originating in the early mother–child relationship, he argues that severe distress in later life often generates a wish to restore the primacy of the one-to-one relationship based on an idealised fantasy of total fusion in the context of a perfectly containing relationship. This is often needed to compensate for profound early disappointment in emotional development, with consequent rage and emptiness. A similar social process creates the notion of an idealised group in which there is total fusion and total containment but this entails a splitting process in which another group – 'the enemy' – is not just denigrated but seen as harbouring destructive intent.

> In terrorist activity, the enemy group is imbued with attributions of great danger, so that annihilation is the only satisfactory solution. This, in turn, enables the 'home' group to strengthen its identification and idealisation as the righteous group. Anti-group attitudes that could impair the cohesion of the home group are no longer a threat to it. The most primitive dynamics of splitting, projection, idealisation and denigration hold sway. (Nitsun, personal communication, 2017)

Hopper (1988) has written about the fear of annihilation caused by traumatic experience, the essence of which is failed dependency and failed holding. He outlined the phenomenology of the fear of annihilation in terms of psychotic anxieties associated with fission and fragmentation, in oscillation with psychotic anxieties associated with fusion and confusion with parts of the self.

Hopper's (1996) notion of 'massification' is helpful in understanding terrorism. This involves members of a group behaving as if they are fused, thereby avoiding any separateness and intimacy. Building on Bion's three basic assumptions, this concept is derived from Hopper's formulation of the fourth basic assumption which he calls 'incohesion' with two distinct manifestations in patterns of interaction, communication, styles of thinking and feeling as well as styles of leadership and fellowship – aggregation and massification (Hopper, p. 151). Groups where traumatic experience is prevalent are likely to be 'incohesive' with an oscillation between aggregation and massification. He uses the metaphor of potatoes to explain these concepts: aggregation is like a bowl of boiled potatoes, each maintaining its identity as an individual potato, whereas massifaction is like a bowl of mashed potatoes where no particular potato can be identified. In other words, in massification the members behave as if they are merged with each other, with an emphasis on their sameness. Hopper believes that this is a group defence against annihilation anxiety, the fear of the total destruction of the self. He emphasises the role of traumatic loss reminiscent of early abandonment or 'total dependency' experiences.

He argues that massification is based on scapegoating which is associated with unconscious shame and guilt that is projected into people and sub-groups who are perceived to be obstacles to perfection and merger with it. They are then banished from the group and deprived of the safety and support available to those who remain in the group.

Hopper explains that the roles generated through incohesion are personified by people who are particularly vulnerable to the suction power of these roles, or who have a valence for the enactment of their demands. Traumatised people who get stuck in states of fission and fragmentation tend to develop crustacean character structures, and people who get stuck in states of fusion and confusion tend to develop amoeboid character structures. The roles generated by aggregation tend to be personified by, for example, crustacean lone wolves, and the roles generated by massification tend to be personified by, for example, amoeboid charismatic narcissists.

De Zulueta (personal communication, 2017) argues that the recurring finding in the literature is that 'terrorists' are essentially normal people who experienced a lack of social ties or attachments. She adds that alienation and shame are the key factors driving Islamic terrorists. She suggests that fundamentalism is about a damaged attachment system due to trauma and that rage in the service of God justifies the deeply held need for revenge, for undoing a hurt by whatever means. Referring to Muslim potential terrorists, De Zulueta (2006) argues that the loss of their cultural and Islamic pride due to centuries of colonialism and exploitation by both the West and by their own leadership is a powerful source of shame and loss of cultural identity, particularly for young men. Fundamentalism thrives on the invalidation by others of what is sacred to those for whom a sense of security and self-respect resides in the rituals and beliefs of their religion. She cites Gilligan's (1996) proposition that the basic cause of violent behaviour is the wish to ward off or eliminate the feeling of shame or humiliation and replace it with its opposite, the feeling of pride. She writes that fundamentalists use sophisticated processes to convert disaffected young men, convincing them that suicide, normally forbidden under Islam, can be a source of glory when carried out for a higher purpose, as a martyr or freedom fighter. She stresses the vulnerability of individuals who have lost their family and community attachments and whose fear of personal psychic annihilation is responded to by those who have the word of God to offer them. He provides the ultimate attachment to those who are desperate. De Zulueta stresses that dehumanisation of the enemy is crucial in terrorism where the dehumanised self is projected on to the 'other' and rage is given freedom of expression.

She warns against punishment and military actions and torture, as the evidence is that these have no deterrent effect and in fact lead to increased violence: 'This is being borne out in Iraq, where even the CIA acknowledges that there will be more extremists as a result of the war' (De Zulueta, 2006, p. 22). She argues that people who feel discriminated against are less likely to approach the police with important information 'which will seriously increase the risk of violence in our country.'

In his plenary lecture to the Group Analytic Symposium in Dublin in 2008, Frosh reported that in contemporary psycho-social theory, the 'neighbour' has become an important topic for investigation. Understood as the 'Other', the neighbour is a key figure in creating the human being as an 'interrupted' subject.

In large groups, the alien nature of the neighbour, who is in essence both close and unknowable, comes to the fore. Participation in a large group can produce a sense of the dissolution of identity, which can be both exhilarating and terrifying, mimicking psychosis.

Referring to Freud's theory of the primal horde, in which identification has spread horizontally as well as vertically, Frosh argues that each individual in the impassioned mob identifies with others who have done the same. The barriers between subjects become porous. Each feels what the other feels: my love and yours entwine, but so, less fortunately, does our hate. We tend to become dislocated from ourselves and connected to others in erotically heightened but also dizzyingly discomforting ways.

Davids (2006) suggests that 'the idea of Islam as the enemy pervades our world today'. Tracing the demonisation of Islam back to 9/11, when the religion itself and its adherents were held responsible for terrorism, he argues that Islamaphobia is an expression of what he sees as internal racism (Davids, 2011). This was mobilised as a defence against widespread annihilation anxiety, which occurred partly in identification with the victims. Davids writes:

> A notion took hold in the collective mind that Islamic terrorists were responsible. This took shape before evidence of the identity of those responsible was available, and before the name 'Al-Qaida' was in circulation. This view revealed the existence in the mind of a heinous figure, a murderous, irrational beast, devoid of anything recognisably human, and his crime was so terrible that it cried out for revenge. Linking the terms 'terrorist' and 'fundamentalist' with 'Islamic' gave an early hint that anti-Islamic strands prevalent within Western culture at large (Runnymede Trust, 1997; Said, 1997) would be gathered together to identify that enemy as the Muslim. (Davids, 2006)

Davids argues that psychoanalytic attempts to understand racism have long recognised the importance of projective mechanisms. Projecting across an us–them divide may be particularly appealing as it allows what is projected to be lodged far from the subject. Following the initial projection, attempts to regulate relationships with the world of the Muslim were inexorably put in place:

> Two wars have been fought in which countless Muslims were killed and their countries' infrastructure ruined, and the 'fundamentalist' heart of Islam has been identified explicitly as the enemy, the headscarf its most visible manifestation. As far as the categories of Islam and Muslim are concerned, there was now little possibility of them being perceived in ordinary human terms.

Dalal (2008) suggests that hate and terror have become synonymous with Islam but it is difficult to talk about because of accusations either of Islamophobia or a naïve and dangerous tolerance. In his paper *Thought paralysis: tolerance, and the fear of Islam*, he asks if he is an apologist for terrorists if he mentions the fact that the war on terror has killed and maimed untold more innocents than all the terrorist attacks and suicide bombings put together. 'I find myself paralysed, because to step anywhere is potentially to cause offence (p. 78.)'

Dalal argues that we homogenise Muslims and thereby damn 'them' all without discriminating between varieties of Islamic belief and practice. He stresses that 'they' are not all the same, and nor are 'we'. 'The Muslim is located outside Europe, and is made container of all that is opposite of the sensibilities that are attributed to Europe ... multiple unconscious denigrations and vilifications continually in play ... the Muslim has become the opposite of the European 'us'. He argues that what is to be feared is the way Islam has been appropriated by some believers, and what they seek to do with it, adding that some of the fear is a paranoid fear born of projection.

Summary of commonalities, insights and theories among the authors

Common themes emerge from the insights and theories of the psychoanalytic and group analytic authors about terrorism. One of the most important is that terrorism is a form of meaningful communication enacted through violence. Many of their ideas centre on shame, humiliation and alienation being driving forces of terrorism.

The importance of past and present trauma and the significance of attachment are seen as central to understanding the complex psychodynamics of terrorism. The aftermath of trauma is often annihilation anxiety and defences of projection are deployed to preserve survival, self-preservation and safety.

Gilligan's (1996) idea that shame is the basic cause of violent behaviour is pivotal in understanding terrorism as a wish to ward off or eliminate shame or humiliation and replace it with its opposite, the feeling of pride. Authors including De Zulueta (1993, 2006, personal communication, 2017), Volkan (1988), Nitsun (1996, personal communication, 2017) and Hopper (1996) refer to the role of shame and humiliation in causing people to react unconsciously to events, rather than reflect, usually due to an inability think, symobolise and communicate verbally.

The social context underpins many of the theories. Akhtar (2002) stresses that a terrorist-prone individual is pushed over the edge by a trigger from the environment which may take the form of an injustice or new trauma to oneself, family or ethnic group. Group analysts Hopper (1988), Nitsun (1991, personal communication, 2017), De Zueleta (1993, 2006, personal communication, 2017) and Blackwell (2012) all refer to the social context.

A central theme is how terrorism may be viewed as a re-enactment of historical trauma that is unresolved, unsymbolised and unspoken. This is Freud's (1920) repetition compulsion whereby the past infiltrates the present – a previous situation is replayed in an unconscious attempt to master the anxieties associated with it. It is the basis of many of the author's theories about undigested experiences from the past being recapitulated in the present. Most psychoanalytic and group analytic writers stress the importance of understanding the impact of previous events and traumas on individual and group identities. Volkan (1997) writes that most major players in a terrorist organisation are deeply traumatised individuals who suffered profound emotional humiliation as children. The same may be said of groups or nations.

This links with the role of attachment. Meloy and Yakeley (2014) refer to Fonagy's proposition that membership of the large group activates the attachment system. De Zulueta (1993) argues that the cause of violence is 'attachment gone wrong' and that 'terrorists' are essentially normal people who experienced a lack of social ties or attachments. She suggests that fundamentalism is about a damaged attachment system due to trauma and that rage in the service of God justifies the deeply held need for revenge, for undoing a hurt by whatever means. Hopper (1988) has written about the fear of annihilation caused by traumatic experience, the essence of which is failed dependency and failed holding. Nitsun's (1991) 'anti-group' concept describes how one group projects its envy, hatred and sadistic fantasies on to another group with the aim of annihilation (Nitsun, personal communication, 2017).

Volkan (1988) highlights the importance of studying large group identity in shaping the terrorist's core individual identity, both being linked to historical traumas and triumphs involving collective pride and shame. These have been unconsciously chosen and ritualised by the group in the service of group cohesion, helping differentiate the group from the enemy.

Both Davids and Dalal refer to hatred being projected across an us–them divide. Davids (2006) suggests that 'the idea of Islam as the enemy pervades our world today', and traces the demonisation of Islam back to the attack on the World Trade Centre when the religion itself and its adherents were held responsible for terrorism. He argues that Islamaphobia is an expression of what he sees as internal racism (Davids, 2011) which was mobilised as a defence against widespread annihilation anxiety, which occurred partly in identification with the victims.

Dalal (2008) suggests that hate and terror have become synonymous with Islam and refers to the 'us and them' mentality whereby Muslims are homogenised and all of 'them' damned cautioning that 'they' are not all the same, and nor are 'we'.

Few psychoanalytic authors write about hope and the search for the good object. Winnicott (1967) referred to delinquency as a sign of hope and the antisocial tendency which is the search for something in the environment which has been lost. Welldon (1997) and Motz (2010) have discussed 'hope' in connection with delinquency and criminality. Hopper (personal communication, 2017) argues that what these authors really mean by hope is a wish to be heard and understood by a good parental figure.

The search for the good object

With regard to the motivation of the terrorist, psychoanalysis often, but not always, focuses on aggression, sadism, hatred and negativity in general, neglecting the more positive aspects of love and the search for the good object. There is often an underlying wish for something better – the aspirational 'dream' of making a 'better world'.

Winnicott (1967) referred to delinquency with respect to the rights and well-being as today what might be described as the 'societal' neighbour and a 'signifier of hope'. He argued that the antisocial tendency is found in children where there has been deprivation – a good early experience has been lost and the environment must compensate for this. Put simply, things went well enough but something disturbed this and the child is yearning for things to be better but is not exactly sure what could be better nor how to achieve that longed for lost state. Two trends are at play in the antisocial tendency – object-seeking and destruction: in the first, the child is looking for something, somewhere and failing to find it seeks it elsewhere, when hopeful; and in the second, there is a search for environmental provision that has been lost (Winnicott, 1984, p. 125). The child instinctively 'wishes' that things could be better as they once were, and unconsciously hankers after it. In other words, these antisocial acts are actually a form of communication – an S.O.S (Winnicott, 1984, p. 116) – and may be a way of testing the environment's capacity to tolerate and understand. There is a crucial message in antisocial behaviour that needs to be decoded – it conveys something to someone in a form which must be heard. If it is unheard and therefore an autistic symptom, it simply remains an act. If it is heard and understood, it realises its potential as a communication. Many minor antisocial acts should be heard as the child's need to try out his 'power to disrupt, to destroy, to frighten, to wear down, to waste, to wangle and to appropriate' (Winnicott, 1984, p. 115).

In the same vein, even an act of violence can be seen as the search for an object relationship associated with self-transformation and repair. Bollas's (1987) notion of the transformational object is helpful in understanding the unconscious longing of the 'terrorist' to commit an act. Stout (2002) quoting Bollas's description of how serial killers re-enact their own experience of annihilation may shed light on understanding how people such as Bin Laden, Hussein and Milosovic resort to such violence. Serial killers had experiences that could be described as soul murder (Shengold, 1979).

Several colleagues, such as Welldon (1997) and Motz (2010), have discussed 'hope' in connection with delinquency and criminality. However, Hopper (personal communication, 2017) argued that what these authors really mean by hope, and what Winnicott seems to have meant by hope, is a wish to be heard and understood by a good parental figure. Many questions remain as to what happens when the good object is found to be bad or when the longing is not met. Does that lead to terrorist rage? Or does the idealisation remain?

Role of the media

No discussion on terrorism would be complete without looking at the media's role. Without attention-grabbing headlines dominating news bulletins, only a small number of people would know that an attack has taken place. Both the media and terrorists need an audience. Research has found that sensationalist media coverage of acts of terrorism results in more such acts being committed (Guardian, 2015).

Bin Laden succeeded with 9/11 attacks by capturing the undivided attention of the world. On the eve of the attacks, he left Kabul for a remote valley in Afghanistan with a convoy of vehicles which included a 'media truck' that had been prepared on his orders. Satellite television receivers and radio antennae in a minivan enabled him to follow news coverage on the BBC World Service as the planned strikes unfolded. The spectacular attacks were replayed on live television again and again. In a few years, this method was outdated by the digital revolution which has altered the way terrorist organisations operate. Daesh has exploited cutting-edge contemporary media to recruit, raise funds and inspire. New technologies have made it possible to produce and disseminate propaganda easily.

Terrorism is Daesh's communications strategy and Western media encourages terrorists through its choice of coverage. Daesh's use of social media marks it out from predecessors such as al-Qaida. But terrorists have always exploited the latest technologies, whether dynamite or digital communications.

Conclusion

In this paper, I have outlined a psychoanalytic and group analytic understanding of the complexity of terrorism and attempted to challenge the demonisation of Islam and homogenising Muslims as though they are all the same without discriminating between varieties of Islamic belief and practice.

Group analysis and psychoanalysis has given helpful insights, especially regarding the driving forces of terrorism such as shame and alienation. There are complex grievances among disaffected people who face poverty and unemployment. Of course, one might argue that the best way of combating terrorism is to narrow the gap between rich and poor. There is also a pernicious effect of social inequality and racism between the powerful and powerless, and the rage that comes with powerlessness.

Acknowledgements

I would like to thank Earl Hopper for his support in writing this paper.

Disclosure statement

No potential conflict of interest was reported by the author.

References

Akhtar, S. (2002). The psychodynamic dimension of terrorism. In C. Covington, P. Williams, J. Arundale, & J. Knox (Eds.), *Terrorism and war: Unconscious dynamics of political violence* (pp. 87–96). London: Karnac Books.

Alderdice, L. (2002). Introduction. In C. Covington, P. Williams, J. Arundale, & J. Knox (Eds.), *Terrorism and war: Unconscious dynamics of political violence* (pp. 10). London: Karnac Books.

Angelou, M. (2014): Gary Younge interview. Retrieved from https://www.theguardian.com/books/2014/may/28/maya-angelou-american-titan-died-86-appreciation

Arundale, J. (2002). Introduction to hatred, enmity and revenge. In C. Covington, P. Williams, J. Arundale, & J. Knox (Eds.), *Terrorism and war: Unconscious dynamics of political violence* (pp. 127–129). London: Karnac Books.

Bollas, C. (1987). *The transformational object in the shadow of the object: Psychoanalysis of the unthought known* (pp. 1–29). New York, NY: Free Association Books, Columbia University Books.

Blackwell, D. (2012). 'Fundamentalism', 'radicalisation' and 'terrorism' revisited: Some notes on the application of group psychotherapy to the understanding of terrorism and political oppression. *Forum: Journal of the International Association for Group Psychotherapy and Group Process, 5*, 69–81.

Dalal, F. (2008). Thought paralysis: Tolerance, and the fear of Islam. *Psychodynamic Practice, 14*, 77–95.

Davids, M. F. (2006). *Internal racism, anxiety and the world outside: Islamophobia Post-9/11*. Keynote lecture given in 2004 to OPUS's International Conference on Organisational and Social Dynamics: Perspectives from Group Relations, Psychoanalysis and Systems Theory, London, published in 2006 (Vol. 6, pp. 63–85).

Davids, M. F. (2011). *Internal racism: A psychoanalytic approach to race and difference*. Basingstoke: Palgrave-Macmillan.

De Zulueta, F. (1993). *From pain to violence: The traumatic roots of destructiveness*. London: Whurr.

De Zulueta, F. (2006). Terror breeds terrorists. *Medicine, Conflict and Survival 22*, 13–25.

Fairbairn, W. R. D. (1952). *Psychoanalytic studies of the personality*. London: Tavistock.

Foulkes, S. (1964/1984). *Therapeutic group analysis*. London: Maresfield Library.

Foulkes, S. H., & Anthony, E. J. (1957/1984): *Group psychotherapy – the psychoanalytic approach*. London: Maresfield Library.

Freud, S. (1920). 'Beyond the pleasure principle'. In J. Strachey (Ed.), *The standard edition of the complete psychological works of Sigmund Freud* (Vol. 18, pp. 1–64). London: Hogarth Press and the Institute of Psychoanalysis.

Frosh, S. (2008). Desire, demand and psychotherapy: On large groups and neighbours, Plenary lecture in Dublin. *Published Psychotherapy and Politics International, 6*, 185–197.

Gilligan, J. (1996). *Violence: Our deadliest epidemic and its causes*. New York, NY: Grosset/Putnam.

Guardian. (2015). *Media coverage of terrorism 'leads to further violence'*. Retrieved from https://www.theguardian.com/media/2015/aug/01/media-coverage-terrorism-further-violence

Hopper, E. (1988). *Psychotic anxieties and society: Fission (fragmentation)/fusion and aggregation/massification*. Cambridge: Lecture for the Royal College of Psychiatry.

Hopper, E. (1996). *Incohesion: (Aggregation/massification): A fourth basic assumption in the unconscious life in social systems*, Public Lecture. London: Centre for Psychotherapy.

Klein, M. (1946/1975). Notes on some schizoid mechanisms. In M. Klein (Ed.), *Envy and gratitude and other works 1946–1963* (pp. 1–24). London: Hogarth Press and the Institute of Psychoanalysis.

Kleinot, P. (2011). Transgenerational trauma and forgiveness: Looking at the Israeli-Palestinian families forum through a group analytic lens. *Group Analysis, 44*, 97–111.

Kohut, H. (1972). Thoughts on narcissism and narcisstic rage. In P. Ornstein (Ed.), *The search of the self.* London: International University Press.

Meloy, R., & Yakeley, J. (2014). The violent true believer as a 'Lone Wolf' – psychoanalytic perspectives on terrorism. *Behavioral Sciences and the Law, 32,* 347–365. Retrieved from wileyonlinelibrary.com. doi:10.1002/bsl.2109

Motz, A. (2010). Self-harm as a sign of hope. *Psychanalytic Psychotherapy, 24*, 81–92.

Nitsun, M. (1991). The anti-group: Destructive forces in the group and their therapeutic potential. *Group Analysis, 24*, 7–20.

Nitsun, M. (1996). *The anti-group: Destructive forces in the group and their therapeutic potential*, International Library of Group Psychotherapy and Group Process. London: Routledge.

Sandler, J. (1987). *From safety to superego*. New York, NY: Guilford.

Sartre, J. P. (1961). Preface to Frantz Fanon's *The wretched of the earth.* Retrieved from: https://www.marxists.org/reference/archive/sartre/1961/preface.htm

Shengold, L. (1979). Child abuse and deprivation: Soul murder. *Journal of the American Psychoanalytic Association, 27*, 533–539.

Stout, C. (2002). *The psychology of terrorism: Vol 1: A public understanding.* Westport, CT: Praeger. Retrieved from: https://books.google.co.uk/books?id=jn2Qn49r5dkC&pg=PA27&lpg=PA27&dq=stout/bollas/the+psychology+of+terrorism&source=bl&ots=6AvE6VwKvn&sig=QpVEcwkGk6lYDj88Hwx2OD-BayA&hl=en&sa=X&ved=0ahUKEwi43tT87fHTAhVIF8AKHfXxAiYQ6AEIJzAA#v=onepage&q=stout%2Fbollas%2Fthe%20psychology%20of%20terrorism&f=false

Trevmow, S. W., & Sacco, F. C. (2002). Reflections on the making of a terrorist. In C. Covington, P. Williams, J. Arundale, & J. Knox (Eds.), *Terrorism and war: Unconscious dynamics of political violence* (p. 107). London: Karnac Books.

Volkan, V. D. (1988). *The need to have enemies & allies: From clinical practice to international relationships*. Northvale, NJ: Jason Aronson.

Volkan, V. D. (1997). *Blood ties: From ethnic pride to ethnic terrorism.* New York, NY: Farrar, Straus, and Giroux.

Volkan, V. D. (1999). Psychoanalysis and diplomacy: Part 1: Individual and large group identity. *Journal of Applied Psychoanalytic Studies, 1*, 29–55.

Welldon, E. V. (1997). Let the treatment fit the Crime: Forensic Group Psychotherapy, Foulkes lecture, published in *Group Analysis, 30*, 9–26.

Winnicott, D. W. (1967). Delinquency as a sign of hope. In C. Winnicott, R. Shepherd, & M. Davis (Eds.), *Home is where we start from: Essays by a psychoanalyst* (1990). Britain: Winnicott.

Winnicott, D. W. (1984). Some psychological aspects of juvenile delinquency and The Antisocial Tendency. In C. Winnicott, R. Shepherd, & M. Davis (Eds.), *Deprivation and delinquency* (pp. 113–131). London: Tavistock.

Fundamentalism, Radicalization and Terrorism. Part 1: terrorism as dissolution in a complex system

John, Lord Alderdice

In the first of two papers in this Special Issue, Lord Alderdice draws on his personal experience of living and working in Northern Ireland and other countries that have suffered from terrorism, and describes from a psychoanalytic and systemic perspective the history of national, cultural and political conflicts which form the backdrop to the struggles against fundamentalism, radicalization and terrorism in current times. By examining and understanding the group dynamics and collective experiences of minority populations that have suffered generations of subjugation, humiliation and injustice at the hands of others, Lord Alderdice demonstrates how terrorism is not an individual but a group phenomenon and that any successful intervention aimed at reducing fundamentalism, radicalization and terrorism needs to identify and take into account the complex relational processes and experiences in all parties involved in the current global conflict.

When many people, including policy-makers and political leaders, in the United States of America were suddenly confronted with terrorism in a new way, they found it difficult to know how to react to the four co-ordinated and catastrophic terrorist attacks by Al-Qaeda in the US on the morning of Tuesday 11 September 2001. There was naturally profound shock and anger at the first major attack on American soil since Pearl Harbour, and it was regarded as a declaration of war and an unjustified and evil assault. It also punctured the sense of security of those who over many generations had come to the United States fleeing wars, revolutions, pogroms and persecution. Now they felt vulnerable in a way that they had not experienced since they or their forebears had arrived. This vulnerability was accompanied by something new. It was not just the fundamentalist way of thinking of these Islamist attackers that seemed so alien to Americans, and indeed to most Europeans too, but also the feelings of hate that were so strong that they drove people not only to kill others but to sacrifice their own lives for a politico-religious purpose, and to feel justified in engaging in terrorist actions that were in contravention of any normal rule of law. In those parts of the world that regard themselves as progressive and secular, at least in the public sphere, where the focus is on improving the individual social and economic well-being of oneself and one's family, where the rule of law is the perceived set of rules for societal behaviour, and where the advancements in science, technology, medicine and communications seem to demonstrate the success of Western thinking, it seemed hard to understand the fundamentalist religious thinking, the radical anti-western impulses and the murderous actions of these terrorist attackers who wanted to wreck and destroy rather than emulate democratic progress.

In such circumstances, in addition to the natural wish to hit back with a hard physical response, people search for a way of making sense of what is happening. It was quickly assumed that there was a linear path connecting these three phenomena. It was described to me by an official in the FBI.

> These people were persuaded of an extreme way of thinking, a distortion of Muslim teachings which we call Islamic fundamentalism. They then became radicalized, probably by some kind of indoctrination by extremists who were anti-West and anti-American, and then they were persuaded to get involved in terrorism.

The outcome of this analysis of a linear trajectory from religious fundamentalism through radicalization to terrorism, was that the authorities believed that if they were going to stop terrorism, in addition to a hard security response, it was necessary to turn this 'extreme thinking' into a more moderate form of religion that stayed safely in the private sphere and contented itself with peaceable relations and thinking more of another world, rather than acting violently in this one. This general analysis has persisted through the various phases of the 'War on Terror', 'Combating Violent Extremism', and now 'Countering or Preventing Extremism'. As the evidence mounted that each phase of this approach was not working and in addition was alienating many moderate Muslims, the tactics changed but they were still informed by the same linear analysis despite it being known that the vast majority of those who hold to their religious faith and practice in a fundamentalist way, do not support the politically motivated violence of Islamist terrorists. The strategy of terrorism, which has been spelt out clearly in written documents from the time of Bakunin and the Russian anarchists through to modern Islamist terrorism is to provoke the state to an overreaction which will split and alienate the community (Naji, 2004). However the response of governments since 9/11 has fallen into this trap and as a result the world is now spinning deeper into a new global conflict.

The Irish Peace Process

Having grown up in Northern Ireland in the 1960s and 1970s there was something familiar about this mistaken approach to terrorism. When my home community broke down again into violence at that time the natural, and in many ways appropriate, response of the Government was to treat the street violence and the subsequent terrorist and paramilitary activity as subversion and a challenge to law and order that needed to be put down with vigorous police and military interventions.

However the outcome was not a resolution of the problem but an escalation of it. In the same way, the military interventions in Afghanistan, Iraq, Libya and elsewhere have not resolved the problem of terrorism. Instead the whole of the wider Middle East and North Africa has descended into chaotic violence and massive social destruction, and international relations in the rest of the world are now worse than at any time since the Second World War.

It is well known that in Northern Ireland, after decades of communal violence, and the failure of many political interventions, a peace process was developed that led to a cessation of violence and the creation of new political institutions, and although these structures are not working as well as they should, no-one expects a return to the campaigns of terrorist violence. We have still substantial political disagreements, but at least we have found a way of disagreeing without killing each other. A good deal has been written about this Irish Peace Process, most of it focusing on the particular history, politics, economics, and religious divisions in Ireland, as well as the new constitutional and institutional arrangements of the 1998 Good Friday Agreement and the work that was done since then on resolving the problems of policing and the administration of justice. These observations tend to point to the particularities of the Irish experience and lead many observers to assume, or even insist, that while it is interesting, it has little relevance for the very different challenges presented by the global Islamist jihadists. There are indeed profound differences in the two contexts, however all such situations involve communities of human beings that cannot get along together. As groups they think, feel and behave in ways that seem impenetrable to outsiders from peaceful stable societies and these disturbances of large group relationships have resulted in apparently intractable violence.

One of the key reasons for the relative success of the Irish Peace Process was that instead of focusing only on the long-lasting divisions of religion and politics and the historic abuses and discrimination, we found new ways of thinking and understanding our problems. This was made possible by changes in the wider context as well as by creativity in the thinking of some of the political leaders. It had become clear that the use of the police, the military and the administration of justice could contain, but not resolve the situation. The Irish Republican Army (IRA) also realized that while they would not be defeated, they could not defeat the British authorities. This led all sides to rethinking at a fundamental level.

The law generally operates at the level of the individual rather than the group. If a crime has been committed the approach of law is to try to identify who was responsible and to take that person through due process to conviction and appropriate sanctions. If the rule of law was not working, could this be because the problem was not essentially one of individuals who broke the law, but was instead a group phenomenon? When we are confronted with lung cancer we do not try to identify why a particular cell has become uncontrollably mitotic rather than any other cell. Instead we deal with the problem at a different systemic level with surgery, radio- and chemo-therapy, and most importantly persuading the population not to smoke. To use another analogy, we cannot understand the operation of an ant colony simply by analysing how each individual ant functions because as a large group new 'emergent' phenomena appear that can only be observed at that 'large group' level. In a similar way, while still implementing the law, we moved away from asking why any particular individual became a terrorist and began to see our troubles as the results of historic disturbed relationships between communities of people. Instead of looking for blame we began to analyse the key sets of disturbed relationships – between Protestants and Catholics within Northern Ireland; between the people of Ireland, North and South; and between Britain and Ireland. The whole of the Irish Peace Process was then built on this analysis, with three strands of talks addressing the three key sets of relationships, involving only those political representatives in each strand of negotiations that were relevant to that set of relationships, and focusing on those issues that related to that set of relationships. This language of relationships was a central feature of the public discourse about the process at that time, though it has tended to be overlooked since. The language of 'relationships' mirrored the systemic ideas that were developing in some approaches to family therapy at that time, but the way that I have found easiest to convey this to people who are not familiar with systems theory or the complexity of large group processes is to tell stories about relationships, because everyone has a sense that this is something they understand, even though in reality there is great complexity involved.

As we had increasing success in this approach to thinking about violent political conflict in the Irish Peace Process, I also explored its application to intractable conflict in other places and worked with colleagues who conducted scientific research by gathering evidence directly from people involved in conflict in various trouble spots (Atran, 2016; Whitehouse et al., 2017). A new paradigm has begun to develop from this work and experience that makes sense of fundamentalism, radicalization and terrorism in terms of what might be called large group psychology.

What makes a terrorist?

Let us go back to that first question people ask when terrorism explodes into their community – 'Why are these people attacking us with this horrible violence?'

The usual answers given in public discourse are that they are either psychologically disturbed, or that they are evil people. However, direct engagement and explorations as a psychiatrist and politician, both inside and outside the therapeutic context in Northern Ireland and elsewhere, has demonstrated to me that most of the people who become involved in terrorism have no prior neurotic or psychotic disorder. Some people develop PTSD and other reactions as a result of their experiences of violence but that is a different matter. Many have grown up in communities where over time the tradition of using physical force to address political problems had developed and their fathers and grandfathers were honoured for their participation in a historic struggle. As a result their involvement in terrorism was an identification with these significant figures. It was ego-syntonic and not an expression of internal conflict. They often described experiences of major trauma where friends or family members were killed or badly injured in bombings, shootings and other violence episodes, and felt that the official institutions – the police, the army and the justice system – gave them and their community inadequate protection or were indeed the instigators of the violence. Others who did not come from parts of the community with a family history of political violence may nevertheless have experienced the same kinds of trauma and found themselves reacting by joining a terrorist or paramilitary organization. This was consciously seen both as a way of joining with others to protect their community and also of satisfying the wish for revenge for their own hurt or the death or injury of their loved one.

These two groups – those who were following a significant tradition (identification with an admired person), and those who joined in a violent response to loss and injury (identification with the aggressor) – often despised another group who appeared to have joined primarily to benefit from the culture of organized crime through which terrorist organizations survive and exert control in their own communities. The largely criminal element seeks to gain personally from extortion, racketeering, drugs and illegal businesses such as the sale of stolen tobacco, alcohol or laundered fuel. These activities are needed by a terrorist organization to raise the substantial funds necessary to conduct an illegal campaign, but the more committed terrorist has a political cause for which they gave up family and financial security and risked their lives. They did not seek personal financial benefit through these illegal activities and resent their political cause being used as a flag of convenience by those whose agenda is crude personal material gain.

After years of active terrorist activity, some of the leaders of the major terrorist organization called the Provisional Irish Republican Army (PIRA) became elected politicians and even ministers in government, and others became community leaders and activists. They acted appropriately, showing care and sensitivity to the needs of the community, and sometimes even of the 'other' community and its leaders. In short, the evidence from the work of those who have actually engaged with people and groups engaged in terrorism is clear. There is no evidential basis for the view that either mental or emotional disturbance or a particular or malign personality type can provide an explanation for why these particular individuals became involved in terrorism.

The political roots of Irish terrorism: a group phenomenon

What then is terrorism, and how and when does it appear? Terrorism usually only breaks out after a lengthy gestation, but once released has its own terrible dynamic as communities begin to think in different ways than when they live in stable peaceful prosperous societies. In Ireland there was a long history of colonial government by Britain, and this not only involved socio-economic disadvantage for Irish people and oppressive political control, but also religious and cultural conflicts. The Anglo-Saxon culture of Britain, and its approach to state and church governance diverged historically from that of Celtic Catholic Ireland which identified more with continental Europe. In the United Kingdom there has recently been a referendum in which England and Wales voted to leave the European Union and Scotland and Northern Ireland voted to remain in the EU. It is worth recalling that this is something of a historic repetition of Henry VIII's decision to leave the Roman Catholic Church, risking not just serious economic consequences, as is the case now, but eternal damnation. The British state survived, as did Anglicanism, but Scotland retained its history of the 'auld alliance' with France, its different legal system and its Presbyterianism, all of which linked it with continental Europe. Ireland as a whole also maintained a more pro-European culture. Ulster identified more with Scotland in its Presbyterianism, which traced its origins to the Low Countries and Switzerland, rather than with England and Anglicanism, and while their loyalty to Britain was intense, it was premised on fact that the same person who wore the Scottish crown also wore the English crown. The Ulster Scots Presbyterians were discriminated against and persecuted by the Anglicans, but the long history of violence in the period of the reformation and counter-reformation and the later merging of Irish Nationalism and Irish Catholicism left Ulster Protestants feeling that there would be greater tolerance for their beliefs and way of life if they remained in the United Kingdom than if they joined in an independent Catholic Ireland.

We know that with individuals we are dealing with personalities that have a persistent way of being-in-the-world. This is not just a set of beliefs about the world, or memories of good or bad experiences. It is a way of perceiving reality and living in relationships. Culture is a large group equivalent of personality. It is the persistent way of 'being-in-the-world' of a large group. It expresses how that community experiences reality and engages in relationships with other large groups. It does not change easily in the face of new experiences and often results in responses to current events that do not make much sense in terms of the 'here-and-now' and are not really appropriate to it. If terrorism is a group phenomenon rather than one of separate individuals how is it similar to and different from the psychology of individuals?

The struggle in Ireland against English hegemony was characterized from at least the eighteenth century on by the adoption and refinement of the tactic of terrorism and by the early part of the twentieth century it enabled the twenty-six southern counties of Ireland to defeat British rule in that part of Ireland and secede from the United Kingdom. Predictably the economic consequences for the Ireland as a whole were not good over the next few generations up until Ireland joined the European Community in 1973, but this never produced any regret about the move to independence. There are some things that cannot be measured in socio-economic terms, and when people engage in terrorism they know that they are not personally likely to be better off, but they are driven by different values, so-called 'sacred values', and believe that their community will benefit by having control of its own affairs and a better sense of esteem. This is why my colleague, Scott

Atran calls them 'devoted actors' who operate on the basis of sacred values in contrast to the so-called 'rational actors' of 'realpolitik' who operate on the basis of socio-economic and power benefits.

While the term 'terror' is used to describe how some authoritarian regimes of both the left and right have tried to control their own people, the term 'terrorism' is usually and most appropriately applied today to the triangular tactic used by those who are less militarily powerful as they struggle against a powerful establishment. Unable to engage in open warfare they attack victims who are entirely innocent, though they may have symbolic significance, because the more powerful government is seen as responsible for their welfare and defence. It is not the victims who are their target, therefore, but rather the responsible government, who the terrorists can show as being unable to defend their own people. The government is then provoked to attack back and often to over-react, both losing their own moral authority and also alienating further the community from which the terrorists have emerged. The power of this tactic may be seen in Ireland where Britain had emerged victorious from the First World War in 1918, but was driven from most of the neighbouring island of Ireland less than four years later, by the IRA led by the utterly committed and tactically shrewd Michael Collins. When he and his colleagues accepted the partition of Ireland as a step towards full independence for the whole island, the anger of those who refused to accept the compromise with Britain resulted in a bitter civil war, and in the newly created entity of Northern Ireland the Catholic nationalists who remained as a permanent minority felt a deep sense of betrayal by their southern co-religionists. They felt no loyalty to the Northern state and the government of Northern Ireland in turn was suspicious of them with the result that the Catholic nationalist community did not integrate and there was discrimination in housing and jobs and unfair treatment of that section of the community.

In the late 1960s when the civil rights marches in the USA offered a new model for effecting change, Northern Irish Catholics came out on to the streets to demand civil rights, and were joined by Protestant liberals and socialists, but there was a violent reaction from the Protestant unionist majority who saw this not just as a demand for civil rights but as an attempt to bring down the Northern Ireland state and force the re-unification of Ireland. This reaction to the civil rights marches blocked the route for potentially peaceful change and opened the path of regression into street riots which quickly deteriorated into vigilantism and then to terrorism with the reappearance and reinvigoration of the IRA which had been dormant since the end of their last unsuccessful terrorist campaign in the late 1950s.

On the Protestant unionist side militias quickly established themselves as defenders of the constitutional status quo, The two largest were known as the Ulster Defence Association (UDA) and the Ulster Volunteer Force (UVF), and by the early 1970s there was widespread bombing of buildings, and huge numbers of fatal shootings by the PIRA, and the UDA and UVF, while the British

Army and the Royal Ulster Constabulary (the Northern Ireland police force) were tasked with maintaining law and order and defeating the terrorist campaigns. The IRA's bombing and shooting campaign was followed in the 1980s with the hunger strikes, the 'armalite and ballot paper' strategy, which combined terrorism with an entry into elected politics, and then came more targeted assassinations and car bombings. By the 1990s there had been a widening of the range of those people who were regarded as 'legitimate targets' for killings, and the strategy of bombing mainland Britain developed. There was deep hatred and division in the community and Northern Ireland politics became ever more polarized. The failure of all of these destructive tactics to bring about a resolution eventually led to the development of a Peace Process involving negotiations amongst all the parties. After the Belfast Agreement in 1998 attacks on security forces and the 'other' side of the community were replaced by attacks on elements in their own side of the community as a way of maintaining control. This too settled as the new agreed political arrangements were gradually put in place and a new way of structuring the community evolved.

How had the rest of the community and the responsible sovereign government in London responded to the regression into terrorist and reactive violence? In the early years of breakdown into gross chaos and mayhem the gruesome and relatively random attacks created widespread acute terror. In the areas of actual street violence the levels of suicide and depression went down, but in the penumbra – the areas around the scenes of violence, which heard the news, and feared what could happen – anxiety mounted and the prescription of benzodiazepines and other psychotropic medication rose considerably. There were demands for a robust security response, resulting in executive detention without trial and vigorous army activity alongside the police. The number of prisoners, soldiers and policemen grew exponentially. Soon there was trouble inside as well as outside the growing prison estate. The prisoners inside, like the community outside, became ever more divided along religious lines and there were major movements of population reflecting this. The communal divisions extended beyond the traditional apartheid in schools and sports activities. People increasingly tended to live, work and socialize only with co-religionists. The territory controlled by each group was clearly marked out by flags and sectarian murals painted on the gable walls of houses. The kerb stones at the edge of pavements were painted red, white and blue in Protestant Unionist areas, and green, white and orange in Catholic Nationalist areas.

This acute phase was gradually replaced by a period of chronic disturbance. The community had regressed from a myriad of individual differences maintained in a broad mosaic of relationships, to a narrower frame of reference where the single difference between Protestant unionist and Catholic nationalist assumed pre-eminence, and was reflected in control of territory. This was physically maintained by attacks on those who crossed the community divide in their personal life, and by regular marches by partisan community groups which marked out the geographical boundaries of the two sections of the community. Only after about thirty years did the many attempts at an exploratory healing process begin to make significant advances towards peace when the British Government came together with the Irish Government and all the parties including Sinn Fein, the political wing of Irish Republicanism (the PIRA being the 'military wing').

From the individual to the group

It will not be difficult to discern in these references to the process of acute dissolution and regression, emergence of primitive phenomena, chronicity, containment (with security containment measures rather than medication or in-patient care) and a slow resistance-bedevilled healing process, something analogous to the breakdown and repair of mental health in an individual. While the way large groups function is not simply a direct read-across from the psychology of the individual, I began to explore how far it was possible to translate the evolutionary or developmental psychoanalytical approach beyond the arena of individual intra-psychic conflict and mental illness into the field of intra- and inter-communal conflict.

While I was doing this from my perspective as a psychoanalytical psychiatrist, some others were using different language to express the same thing. John Hume, the leader of the Social Democratic and Labour Party, a largely Catholic nationalist party which was fervently against the use of violence for political ends, had closely observed the process of European integration after the Second World War, and understood that while social and economic cooperation were the tools of the European project its purpose was to ensure peace in Europe after the terrible experiences of repeated and devastating wars. He also appreciated that the question was not whether individual people had good relationships, but whether the large groups to which they belonged had good relationships with each other. The violence was therefore seen by us and people like us as a disturbance of relationships between these large groups and that these disturbed relationships needed to be understood and addressed.

The notion that we should try to achieve some understanding of people and groups involved in politically motivated violence is a challenge to the simple law and order approach. The immediate emotional response to a terrorist campaign of splitting the community into bad (the terrorists who are outside the pale) and good (law-abiding citizens who need protected from them) was clearly observable in Northern Ireland where it deepened divisions between Protestants and Catholics, less over the acceptability of terrorism than about whether the government attempts to deal with it were justified, proportionate and appropriate. Similarly in the global 'War on Terror' after 9/11, while the terrorists were partially isolated, those who proclaimed the war against them also increasingly experienced antagonism from erstwhile allies because of their military reaction to the terrorist campaign. The result was that instead of being seen as successful defenders of their people from the evils of terrorism most of the political leaders of the 'War on Terror' departed the political scene with the mark of failure and with their reputations for moral leadership damaged and permanently stained. Meanwhile those terrorist leaders who have not been killed are unmoved in their determination, and the strength and depth of the hatred involved on all sides continues to overcome any rational appreciation of the damage of the constantly expanding war which is self-evidently not in the interests of either individuals or society. Rational argument is a weak lever in the face of profound violence and hate, and in any case splitting into good and bad and making the struggle into a moral one of good against evil is the exercise of a psychological defence mechanism against profound anxiety rather than a result of rational psychologically-informed analysis. It is also a very particular way of thinking which does not engage with the complexity involved.

Another kind of 'good/bad split' that has been adopted by some analysts proposes that terrorism is a result of inequality and post-colonial poverty. Of course there is a moral imperative to address the painful inequalities of education, health and economic well-being in the world, however it is generally not when societies are at their poorest that they fall victim to the tactic of terrorism. Northern Ireland began to experience terrorism as Catholic grievances were actually being addressed by a more progressive Protestant unionist government in the late 1960s. The Middle East became more unstable after oil was discovered there. Mr Osama bin Laden was not a poor man, indeed he came from an element in the more wealthy Saudi elite. What he did demonstrate in his personal life was much of the experience of humiliation and disrespect which I have found to be the emotional driving forces in the group dynamic behind the involvement in terrorism (Robinson, 2001). That it is not in the depths of deprivation, but at the point of improvement that things become most vulnerable to breakdown suggests that the link with socio-economic disadvantage and emotional reaction comes from a sense that the relative disadvantage is experienced as unfair. This is not just a reaction to current experiences, but may be a sustained and historic sense of injustice which survives long after the actual period of traumatic unfairness is past and the context has completely changed. As we found out in Northern Ireland, simply improving current socio-economic conditions does not resolve the problem. Where people believe that their relative disadvantage is the result of poor education or social or cultural differences they may even accept these as unhappy but justifiable causes of their disadvantage. When their educational opportunities improve and they feel as capable as the next person, they begin to see their disadvantage more in terms of historic cultural, racial or political discrimination. The next step is to try to change this by peaceful political means, but when non-violent options are exhausted the use of physical force comes on to the agenda. This relatively rational explanation for the emergence of violence as a last resort could be seen as a 'realpolitik' of the left.

Those on the right who espouse what is more commonly referred to as 'realpolitik' attempt to give a rational analysis of what national leaders or their countries perceive to be in their own best interests, and propose responses of a simple behavioural kind, giving economic and political favours as encouragement, and embarking on punitive operations and war to discourage negative behaviour. The approach of the Bush administration to the wider Middle East, and Israeli attacks on Palestinians in Gaza and the West Bank could be seen as being characterized by this approach to the problem. This will not work as an explanation nor have the actions that have flowed from it been successful in putting down the violent threat, and this should not be surprising to us since we know from our clinical experience that individuals and groups often act against their own best interests, especially when their emotions are high.

Disrespect, humiliation and injustice

As I came to develop personal relationships with those who represented the different strands of group life in the politics of Ireland, North and South I was struck by how the strength of their feelings was associated with powerful communal memories of times when their group, or they as representative individuals of their group, had been disrespected or humiliated. These experiences provoked deep anger and created a capacity for responses at least as violent as those that had been experienced. When these problems of institutionalized humiliation and unfairness were not able to be resolved by democratic politics because of the inbuilt majority of Protestant unionists and when the civil rights marches of the 1960s failed to make the necessary changes, there was a breakdown again into terrorism.

Subsequently I have explored whether this triad of the sense of unfairness/injustice, humiliation/disrespect and the failure of peaceful democratic attempts to right the perceived wrongs, was only related to the outbreak of terrorism in Northern Ireland, or whether there are similar underlying patterns in other countries that have experienced violent insurgencies. Let me briefly give a few examples.

In Peru there is a historic and, despite recent elections, a current failure by the descendants of the Spanish conquistadors to integrate the majority native population into the mainstream of establishment life. They remain generally poor, but also disrespected and excluded from positions of power. This was borne in on me some years ago as I participated in a ceremony when the remains of seven of the tens of thousands of those 'disappeared' during the Sendero Luminosa (Shining Path, Maoist) terrorist insurgency were returned to their families. As I walked with the families through the streets of Ayacucho following the coffins, few people paid any attention. They just went about their business ignoring this multiple funeral. These grieving people and their dead relatives seemed to be of no import; they were split off and disregarded. It is worth noting that despite the defeat of Sendero Luminso, the politics of Peru remain disturbed.

In Nepal – the last Hindu kingdom – the upper castes in power excluded the lower castes from positions of respect, and split the community into 'good' and 'bad', with the same toxic humiliation I had identified previously. When the limited moves to democracy were abandoned the representatives of the ordinary people then espoused a violent Maoist strategy, but only after any democratic prospect was removed. They subsequently engaged in a peace process which brought an end to the monarchy and Prachandra the leader of the Maoists became Prime Minister of the new republic.

One thing that is striking about Nepal, Peru and Northern Ireland is that despite their angry, violent promotion of the cause of the oppressed, the terrorist treatment and abuse of their own people during the struggle was appalling. Their lack of humanity in the treatment of those in whose cause they fought, powerfully points up that it is not merely a rational, sympathetic response to the socio-economic plight of the poor. I had been very much aware of this at home where the Roman Catholic nationalist community suffered more from the PIRA campaign than did the Protestant unionist community, and when I became involved in the Arab/Israel conflict and especially with the problems for Palestinians, I found all the same things. Here was a community that felt humiliated and unfairly treated, and that came to believe that there was no peaceful way of resolving their problems. The result of them turning to violence certainly inconvenienced their Israeli enemies, but the people who suffered most from their violent struggle were their own people. I should say that it was also very clear to me that Jewish Israelis also carried with them a profound sense of historic humiliation, disrespect and unjust and profoundly unfair treatment and a belief that only the use of force could protect them in the future, so this triad can affect more than one community in any conflict.

Although the situations in Northern Ireland, Peru, Nepal and Israel/Palestine are widely divergent when assessed on economic, historical and political grounds, all experienced violent terrorist campaigns which had emerged in the context of a long-standing sense of injustice and humiliation felt by a significant section of the population. There was also a deep feeling of shame connected to a sense of the failure to protect, repair or resolve the injustice and unfairness of their circumstances. These feelings were personal but also communal, and experienced as a loss of power or agency, with the terrible feeling of being wiped out. However, adopting the tactic of terrorism can hardly been seen as a simple rational choice of strategy since it has been tried in many parts of the world and while it has only been successful in a few situations, it has inevitably been much more destructive of the community from which it emanates that of the community that they see as the enemy. A rational individual reaction model is much less helpful in explaining this self-damaging outcome than one which would take account of the processes of evolution and dissolution in the group and the power of emotions in the causation of political terrorism.

Is it the case that young people have espoused Islamist terrorism because they have adopted extreme religious ideas that provoke them to engage in terrorism?

Research interviews conducted by my colleagues with young people in the Middle East and North Africa show that they had little intellectual understanding of Islamic theology, and much of what they did know they had absorbed after their involvement in terrorist groups, or even after their imprisonment for terrorist offences. This suggests that their engagement was not a result of a primary cognitive commitment to a religious-political programme. Indeed for many it was not so much recruitment by the godfathers of terrorism but, as Sageman (2004) and Atran (2006) have shown, voluntary enlistment with friends with whom they may have played football or had family connections.

Analysts of terrorism have often attempted to differentiate between the kind of terrorist insurgencies associated with nationalistic struggles and the conflict between Islamists and the West which is seen as more irrational, fundamentalist and not open to engagement. However in my own experience of meeting and talking extensively with leading figures in Hamas and Hezbollah in the Middle East over a number of years it has been clear that as far as they are concerned the same key problems are present – severe relative deprivation, a deep sense of injustice especially (but not only) on the question of land, experiences of humiliation and disrespect and a belief that all non-violent options have been exhausted. In that sense those movements in Palestine, Lebanon and the surrounding region are movements whose purpose is to right perceived wrongs on behalf of their own people. In so far as they have turned to co-religionists for help it is in the service of this primary purpose rather than their being primarily instruments of a wider malign conspiracy or a result of their fundamentalist theology. However the more they see no peaceful route to resolving the historic as well as the current hurt and grievance of their people and instead experience sanctions and exclusion, the more their people regress into destructive and self-destructive thinking and actions and see their difficulties as being not only a problem of their own local community but as they fuse with the wider Muslim world they see their problems as a local version of a global humiliation and injustice against Muslims.

In the early days of my engaging with Hamas and Hezbollah it seemed possible that if an alternative route could be opened up, an evolution towards a peaceful outcome could slowly be found, as had been the case in South Africa and Ireland. However all attempts to achieve this were frustrated by other forces and now I am not optimistic that there is any intention of opening up a route for the peaceful resolution of this conflict. What is certain is that the mere passage of time, attempts to destroy the extremist ideology of such groups, and the killing of individual leaders have not been successful and will not be successful in expunging their feelings of humiliation and injustice. The reasons behind the adoption of the tactic of terrorism are the failure to deal with the disturbed historic relationships between groups of people, as well as the resultant feelings and memories that are passed from generation to generation and the power differentials that ensure that more open confrontation is not viable. This suggests that terrorism is not a result of extremist thinking but a reaction to extreme emotions, specifically the feelings association with humiliation and profound unfairness, and the obstruction of their resolution through peaceful democratic engagement.

The continuation of the complex I have described will lead to deepening regression. As Khaled Mashal, the leader of Hamas at the time, put it to me, 'Israel and the West does not have to engage with us, but they should understand that we are prepared to work the system and to stand for elections. If we are unsuccessful we will be in opposition and if we are elected to government we will govern. You may not like how we will govern, but it will be the way approved democratically by our people. If the US and Israel do not engage with us there are others coming after us who do not want to work the system; they want to burn the system'. This was the first clear indication to me of the rise of ISIS and others of that kind, and the subsequent course of events proved him right. Failure to engage with the concerns of the Palestinian people, led to the rise of the PLO. Failure to create real progress with the PLO led to the rise of Hamas. Failure to engage with Hamas leads to the rise of other more extreme and regressed manifestations.

Group processes and globalization: the current picture

This leads us to the large group psychological processes at work in the emergence of the global jihadist networks of Al Qaeda, the Islamic State and others. At one level one could observe that a combination of the collapse of the Soviet Union and the 'stable instability' of the Cold War led to regression, with the re-appearance of old nationalisms and religious divisions that had been kept under wraps for many years. In particular, the long-standing resentments of the Muslim world at the defeat and destruction of the Ottoman Empire and the ending of the Caliphate in the early years of the twentieth century had been simmering for decades and all attempts to build more progressive democratic structures had been frustrated by Western interventions and support for authoritarian regimes in the region. In addition, since humanity has not yet found a way of living without an enemy, the collapse of 'the familiar enemy', the Soviet Union, led to the emergence of Islamism not only *sui generis*, but also, one could argue, as an unconscious result of the need of the West for a new enemy.

Added to these challenges, globalization, consequent on technological developments in communication, travel, and weapons of mass effect has produced profound group anxiety and a regression in societal thinking towards religious and non-religious fundamentalism and culturally to old societal themes and structures that appeared to provide people with some reassurance of certainty. The reaction is complex because of the deep ambivalence to the West where, mixed with antipathy towards its dominance and intrusion, there is a wish to possess some of the benefits of education, healthcare and economic prosperity represented by Europe and more especially its offspring, the United States of America. There is also the haunting puzzle of why their Islamic society which was once fertile in ideas and innovation has suffered such reversals and humiliation. Part of the political answer given by Islamists is that it is not just western imperialism, but what they see as Muslim betrayal in the form of the Arab royal families and the regimes in Egypt and elsewhere holding on to and enjoying the oil wealth and power from their alliance with the West rather than sharing these resources with their own people. The hypocrisy, as it is seen, of Western powers proclaiming an attachment to democracy and human rights while allying themselves with undemocratic governments and disregarding the results of free and fair elections, adds to the sense of shame, humiliation, injustice and deep anger and the dangerous possibility of a regression beyond the split between Islam and the West into the communal split and sectarian bitterness of Shiite against Sunni.

It is important to note that the regression into fundamentalism, and the sense of humiliation and injustice are also present in Europe and the United States of America. Some of the same angry feelings are felt in their populations too, and fundamentalism on the right and the left is also an increasing characteristic of thinking in those regions. A key difference is that in the West democracy gives an opportunity to express those frustrations by changing the government and shape of the polity, as evidenced by Brexit in the UK and the election of Donald Trump as President in the USA. As much as these events provoke extremes of outrage, jubilation and adulation, such emotive responses, albeit involving significant proportions of the population, have not degenerated into the large group regressive processes that result in violence. In less contained parts of the world, where populations differentiated by ethnicity, religion or ideology are marginalized or persecuted, and change through peaceful democratic means is blocked and frustrated, violent conflict becomes the only language that is heard, and is often more a communication of angry despair, than a considered strategy for change. It is only through attempts to understand and address their collective history of traumas, injustices, humiliations and grievances that continue to be so strongly felt, that another language of more peaceful engagement may emerge and prevent the ongoing intergenerational transmission of fundamentalism, radicalization and terrorism.

Disclosure statement

No potential conflict of interest was reported by the author.

ORCID

John, Lord Alderdice http://orcid.org/0000-0003-4322-0049

References

Atran, S. (2006, April 28). Global network terrorism, briefing to National Security Council, White House. Retrieved from https://www.sitemaker.umich.edu/satran/files/atran_nsc_042806.pdf; https://www.au.af.mil/au/awc/awcgate/whitehouse/atrannsc-042806.pdf

Atran, S. (2016, June). The devoted actor: Unconditional commitment and intractable conflict across cultures. *Current Anthropology, 57*, S192–S203. doi: 10.1086/685495

Naji, A. B. (2004). *The management of savagery: The most critical phase through which the Umma will pass*. (W. McCants (2006), Trans.). Cambridge, MA: John M Olin Institute for Strategic Studies at Harvard University.

Robinson, A. (2001). *Bin Laden - Behind the mask of the terrorist*. Edinburgh: Mainstream Publishing.

Sageman, M. (2004). *Understanding terror networks*. Philadelphia: University of Pennsylvania Press.

Whitehouse, H., Jong, J., Buhrmester, M. D., Gómez, Á., Bastian, B., Kavanagh, C. M., … Gavrilets, S. (2017). The evolution of extreme cooperation via shared dysphoric experiences. *Scientific Reports, 7*, 44292. Retrieved from http://www.nature.com/articles/srep44292.pdf

Fundamentalism, Radicalization and Terrorism. Part 2: fundamentalism, regression and repair

John, Lord Alderdice

Prior to the watershed events of 11 September 2001, terrorism was generally seen simply as politically motivated, criminal violence. Since then the phenomena of religious fundamentalism, political radicalization and terrorism have become fused in the public mind, partly under the influence of the political and military reaction described as the 'War on Terror' and its successors. While there is clearly an important overlap in the religious thinking of some fundamentalists, the radical agenda of political Islamist groups and the violent activities of those who currently use the tactics of terrorism, these are not identical phenomena, and treating everyone who falls into one of these groups as the same as all the others has exacerbated rather than improved global security. In the second of two papers based on his work with terrorist organizations and areas of the world embroiled in entrenched conflict, Lord Alderdice develops a different approach informed by psychoanalytical principles and systems and complexity theories to clarify some of the boundaries and overlapping elements of these three phenomena. This approach not only provides a more evidence-based analysis, but also permits a more reflective and constructive response to these clear and present dangers.

Psychotic processes

Many years ago, when I shared with my friend, Estela Welldon, my observations about the importance of humiliation and disrespect in the emergence of terrorist violence, she drew my attention to how reminiscent they were of the work of Gilligan (1996) with mentally disturbed individuals who had committed serious violent crimes in the United States. He had made observations about what he described as 'shaming' in prisoners who had subsequently committed very violent crimes against other persons, similar to what I have described in the origins of the terrorism in various parts of the world. Despite the awfulness of their crimes his prisoner patients also believed themselves to be justified; righting some terrible wrong; some deep disrespect done to them. This is similar to those groups that engage in terrorism. While the rest of the world may see them as evil, they believe that theirs is a moral and courageous activity motivated not by personal material gain but by principle. They do it, not because they have weighed up the balance of cost and benefit to themselves but because they believe that they are making costly sacrifices to do what is right and obey the will of Allah. Those against whom they pit themselves are seen as the immoral ones and they cite not only political oppression, but also the falling away of a sense of meaning and moral purpose and commitment in the West, a critique which they would actually share with some Christian fundamentalists and others in the West.

Gilligan's patients were individuals suffering from psychoses. This is not the case with individual terrorists, because there is no evidence of individual mental disturbance and indeed, terrorist groups exclude those with serious mental disorders because of the risk they create for the group, but is it possible to interpret the disturbances of thinking of their group as analogous to the psychotic process in an individual?

Some see psychotic thinking as a regression to ways of mental functioning in early childhood and there are clearly aspects of that. However, there are forms of mental functioning in psychosis which are not seen in childhood in any demonstrable way. Freud (1911) described this as primary process thinking and observed it not only in dreaming but also in the process of psychosis. Is it possible that there is an analogous form of thinking which is not just a return to how a community has functioned in the past, but is a change to a different 'primary process' type of thinking which is not arising in isolated individuals but at the level of the group?

Certainly members of terrorist groups present a mode of thinking which is different from the more 'rational actor' whose behaviours are driven by calculations of utility and cost/benefit analysis. The terrorist is a devoted actor motivated by moral imperatives, resistant to material trade-offs and normative social influence. In addition, the sharing of painful and high emotional experiences produces 'identity fusion' – a visceral sense of oneness – which in turn can motivate self-sacrifice, including the willingness to fight and die for the group. Their values become fused with those values in their group, and they not only willingly dedicate themselves to protect the group and its values but make costly sacrifices and take extreme actions (Whitehouse et al., 2017).

There is also a denial in word and action of the individual humanity of those who are about to suffer at their hands. The perception of the people who will die in the Twin Towers or a bomb in Belfast or Tel Aviv is that they are Americans, Protestants or Catholics, or Jews, and that this is all that is to be said. Just as in psychotic thinking the part stands for the whole and the complexity, humanity, individuality and difference of the other is lost. There is a loss of appreciation that those they kill may not be their enemies. They may not as individuals share the position of their government or state and may even have campaigned for the cause espoused by the terrorist who will now kill them, but this is lost from thinking. They are set aside as the 'unfortunate collateral damage of war'. In using such a phrase, we immediately become aware that the need to set aside the individual humanity of the victim of our violence is also a necessary defence for all soldiers including those who respond militarily to terrorist attacks with orders to 'destroy the terrorists'. The attachment to a hard won rational system of law and liberal democracy is always in danger of being loosened by the powerful emotions unleashed in the community by the terrifying nature of terrorism. Terror is a result of the regression into violence, but it is not a mere side effect of these attacks. It is also their purpose not just to blow away people and buildings but also the institutional and mental structures of freedom and order that a group worked for centuries to put in place. An angry terrorism often provokes an emotional response rather than a calculated one and such responses can destroy that which they wish to protect.

Dissolution, regression and reparation

While speaking of the processes of evolution and dissolution, and disturbances of thinking and behaviour as regression are reminiscent of the thinking of Freud and other psychoanalysts, their use of these ideas emerged from the earlier work of Hughlings Jackson, the father of neurology (Critchley & Critchley, 1998). Jackson (1887) described how as individuals we develop physically by evolving from the simple, predictable reflexes of the early period to more complex, adaptive responses. However, he also showed how in later times when there was trauma or disease and the inhibitions which enabled the greater complexity of the higher functions were damaged, there was not only a loss of the higher functions, but also a return or release of the earlier reflexes and then a reparative process emerging from the remaining capacities. He later applied the same model to what we could call a higher systemic level, that of mentation, and showed how in mental illnesses there was also a loss of higher functions and return of more primitive mental life. It was this that Freud took as the model for his own theoretical reflections. When Jackson (1887) was trying to describe the processes of evolution and dissolution in neurological development and disease in the individual, he actually used the analogy of the group –

> The higher nervous arrangements evolved out of the lower keep down those lower, just as a government evolved out of a nation controls as well as directs that nation. If this be the process of evolution, then the reverse process of dissolution is not only a 'taking off' of the higher, but is at the very same time a 'letting go' of the lower.

It seemed to me that we could, indeed, apply an analogous model of evolution and dissolution at the systemic level of the large group, but Freud was not the only one to develop a theory based on Jacksonian thinking.

Henri Ey, the great French psychiatrist, developed a neo-Jacksonian approach which he called organo-dynamic because it paid due attention to both biological and psychological aspects of psychiatry, and was congruent with both (Ey, 1962). The key features of this model are his explication of mental life as being our construction of 'reality' and his application of the development/regression model to that experience of reality. He takes the phenomenological approach of Edmund

Husserl and Martin Heidegger and applies it within a neo-Jacksonian framework. He describes how as we develop in the first few months and years we begin to evolve the capacity to differentiate between memories of the past, experience of the present and hopes and fears for the future. He describes this as the temporal function. Similarly, we develop a spatial capacity to distinguish between what is inside me and what is outside me. These temporo-spatial capacities are developmental achievements through which we experience reality more nearly as it is. He saw mental illness as a disturbance of this capacity of experiencing reality in time and space. As a result, we may experience in the here-and-now things that have already happened in the past or we may experience our own thoughts as the voices of other people speaking. Mental disturbance results in a 'disease of reality' and our experience of it. In the regression or dissolution of the experience of reality, whatever the cause, there are negative features coming from the loss of higher functions, as well as positive symptoms coming from the release of the remaining mental functions, but there is also reconstructive or reparative work which follows, over time. Such regressions may be sudden, temporary mental crises, or may become chronic in which case there are adaptations or reconstructions of the personality from the remaining and regressed or lost capacities. The negative effect of the illness involves the loss of the temporal capacity to distinguish in the experiencing of time what is past, present and future, and with loss of the spatial function a loss of differentiation between what is inside me and what is outside me and part of someone else.

Henri Ey also differentiated between two different pathologies – that of the 'field of consciousness' and that of personality. The latter is a regression of the historical construction of the self. In the former, he is describing a dissolution of the way in which consciousness is experienced. As I noted earlier there are forms of mental functioning in psychosis which are not seen in childhood. Ey seems to be referring to the appearance of this primary process thinking in dreaming, delirium and psychosis.

Just as ordinary people speak of mental illness as 'crazy' and regard it as impossible to understand, people from stable peaceful parts of the world find it difficult to make sense of the continued living out of the past and the disturbed way that people who live under threat experience the world. However, if we apply such a phenomenological model to large-group identity, we can see the temporal regression or 'collapsing of time' such that events from the distant past may evoke powerful images and emotions, as though they happened only yesterday. As a group develops it begins to have the capacity to set down and recall its history in terms of historic traumas or victories from the past, and to hope for better in the future. When a group feels under existential threat, however, it may lose the capacity to differentiate history from the here-and-now, continuing to live in the experience of hundreds of years ago. Such a community has lost the capacity to treat the past as history and to set down a psychological boundary between it and the present (and the future). Parades in Northern Ireland that used to be commemorative of past victories, came to be experienced as a part of a current struggle, and past traumas were lived as though inflicted by the current generation of their historic enemies.

Some communities not only regress to a previous experience of time but also, with a loss of confidence in control of place (the spatial function for the group) become concerned about who is in their group and who is not. In Northern Ireland, kerb stones were painted with the colours of each community (red, white and blue for the British flag, and green, white and orange for the Irish flag) and other physical markers were used as identifiers of the boundaries of the community. The loss of spatial function in the individual is experienced in primary process thinking, both in dream life, from which we can voluntarily waken up, and also in the more terrifying psychotic loss of ego boundaries, characterized, for example, with the release phenomena of transitivism and appersonation and the appearance of hallucinations, where the patient's thoughts or memories or even boundaries of their physical bodies and those of others are confused. Sometimes the feeling of dissolution of the self is actually experienced directly in psychosis or in the pre-psychotic period. Various attempts are made by the remaining mental function to make sense of the experience, or repair the 'reality', for example, through delusion formation.

The importance of boundaries

Applying this to the large group, whatever the cause, regression would involve a loss of the higher functions which enable history to be experienced as past (temporal function), and problems emerge about differentiation between the group and other groups (spatial function). The loss of these boundaries leads to the collapse of time so that the past invades the present, and the loss of differentiation between individual people and between the large group and other large groups leads to what another French intellectual, Rene Girard calls a 'mimetic crisis' with the attendant danger of violence (Girard, 1977).

In human beings says Girard, there are not only the instinctual appetites for food, water and so on, which we share with the animal kingdom, but also imitative desire – 'I want that because I observe that you have it'. This fundamental mechanism of mimesis or non-conscious imitation of desire inevitably leads to rivalry and in Girard's view the social constructions of law, culture and religion were essentially mechanisms that set down boundaries for rivalry, which, if uncontrolled, would lead by rapid mimesis to a violent rivalrous crisis. The particular device at the centre of this boundary setting is the scapegoat mechanism, by which, instead of everyone being set against everyone in violence, all turn against one individual who is demonized, victimized, sacrificed, and then, since his sacrifice brings peace, is ultimately divinized. Girard identifies this mechanism as key to understanding the foundational myths of what he calls archaic religions. In every repetition of the phenomenon, the lynch mob feels itself justified in their violence against this individual who is regarded as the embodiment of some sort of evil. The difference between such myths and Judaeo-Christian religion in particular (as exemplified in the crucifixion of Christ and its ritualization in the Eucharist) is, he says, the recognition that the identified victim is actually innocent and that he is being sacrificed, not because of his wickedness, but to rid the community of its violence. The problem is that once the myth of the wickedness of the victim is exposed as a lie the power of the mechanism is destroyed for no-one can feel so justified in 'scapegoating'. In a post-9/11 expression of his thinking, Girard (2005) says that while the realization of the hypocrisy or 'lie' behind the scapegoat mechanism has ensured that we have in many ways become less violent through our insistence on the rights of women, racial and religious minorities, the disabled and other victims or potential victims, this demythologizing has also contributed to more violence through the release of the old mimetic violence which the sacrificial violence was instigated to control.

The implication of Rene Girard's approach is that it is not religion that is the cause of violence (not even fundamentalist religion though it is also along a regressive road) but the breakdown of the boundaries established through culture, religion and law that results in the release of violence, that is to say it is the failure of religion to contain the violence that is the problem. This argument implies that after the breakdown of the horrible but stabilizing boundary of the Cold War, the emergence of a new and peaceful world order depended on putting new boundaries in place. Without that, the positive opportunities of globalization, with its freedom to trade, travel and communicate could only be perceived as a threat. The current regression to fundamentalist ways of thinking in the West as well as the East is then a flight from and defence against this modernity in the absence of other more healthy defences. The Islamists make this clear when they proclaim that the solution is for the great evil which is America to leave their part of the world, that is to say, for a new East/West boundary to be established. This is a profound and dangerous regression, but without alternative boundaries such as those set by the United Nations and international law, reciprocal violence seems almost inevitable. However, we know that fundamentalism itself does not inevitably lead to violence. Is this only because it naturally leads to a separation off into different cultures, thinking, rules and ways-of-being that establish boundaries between groups and so manage the mimetic danger?

Professor Vamik Volkan, a psychoanalyst who has worked with many political and religious groups in areas of conflict, has identified 10 common characteristics of what he calls 'encapsulated' fundamentalist groups – a divine text; an absolute leader who is the interpreter of the divine text; a demand for total loyalty to the group and the yielding up of all aspects of life and choice to the group and its leader; tangible benefits for members; feelings of being both omnipotent and yet victimized; extreme sadistic and/or masochistic acts; alteration of the shared 'morality'; creation of borders (psychological and sometimes physical) between the group and the rest of society; changing of family, gender and sexual norms within the borders; and negative feelings and fear amongst outsiders (Volkan, 2008). These 10 observations from 'encapsulated' fundamentalists are clearly not entirely separable items. The setting down of a border for the group and the creation of different ways of thinking and behaving based on the divine text as (idiosyncratically) interpreted by the single inspired leader will not surprisingly contribute to the sense of omnipotence, the negative attitudes of outsiders, and the resultant and ambivalently unwelcome sense of victimization.

Volkan further postulates that when for some reason a significant number of outsiders begin to become sympathetic rather than have negative feelings about the group, perhaps because the wider society has undergone a massive trauma that has resulted in feelings of humiliation and helplessness, the idea of a 'saviour' becomes attractive. He refers to the remarkable growth and power of the Taliban in post-Soviet Afghanistan and describes as especially powerful the symbolic link established with Mohammed through the leader, Mulla Omer, publicly putting his arms into the sleeves of a cloak believed to have belonged originally to the prophet Mohammed – this symbolic link collapsing the passage of time and the separateness of the two individuals concerned. While the eminent Islamist scholar and Pakistan Senator, Professor Khurshid Ahmad has disputed the authenticity of reports of this particular event, Volkan has demonstrated a similar mechanism in a number of other case studies in the Balkans, the Baltic states, Cyprus and elsewhere.

Large-group identities

Volkan also sees the phenomenon of fundamentalism as representing a regression in the functioning of a group in the face of a threat or threats to the identity of the large-group, an idea that he has developed out of a revision of Erik Erikson's description of individual identity (Erikson, 1956). Large-group identity – whether it refers to religion, nationality, ethnicity or shared ideology – he defines as the subjective experience of thousands or even millions of people who are linked by a persistent sense of sameness, while also sharing some characteristics with 'others' who belong to foreign groups. He describes this identity as being part of the psychic development of the large group which emerges out of its, often mythologized, history, and describes how, in a fashion analogous to that of the individual under threat, it is possible for the large group to regress to points in its earlier development where chosen glories and traumas (analogous to fixation points) become infused with emotion and significance and lead to a series of defences. An example would be the appearance in a people of 'entitlement ideologies' such as irredentism where the nation's difficulty in mourning the loss of people, land or prestige, in, for example, the loss of empire, leads to attempts to deny the losses and seek to recover them either in fact or in symbolic form, sometimes at great cost, and with a continuing significance that is not much diluted by time, and can be re-ignited after years or even centuries. Another example are the 'purification' practices where words are purged from a language, symbols removed from view, or worst of all, ethnic cleansing is embarked upon, to repair the damaged sense of identity, in a defence analogous to externalization/projection in the individual. (Volkan, 2006).

One of the important things about Volkan's work is that he not only applies the concept of identity to the large group but he also sites it within an evolutionary or developmental process, which can be put into reverse in the context of trauma. He notes, however, the importance of the infusion of emotion. Is this the place where we begin to see an important differentiating factor between fundamentalism and the process of radicalization that results in terrorism?

Where there is a sense of threat to the identity of the group, such as the existential threat provoked by all the different kinds of global uncertainties identified above, the regression will take the form of loss of functions which had developed to deal with complexity and a re-emergence of more simple, predictable, reactive ways of thinking and behaving as a group. This provides a sense of clarity and certitude, albeit about things of which no-one can in truth be certain, but the anxiety is reduced. One 'knows' that one is doing 'the right thing' whether or not this is truly the case.

Fundamentalists and violent jihadists do not generally see their movements as merely going back to the past. They certainly believe that they are identifying key strands from the roots of their faith and tradition, which they feel to have been overlooked, lost or denied, however, they describe their activities as 'revival', and many readily espouse new technology in their own lives. Ahmad (2006) starts his paper on Jama'at-e-Islami in precisely this way, and in conversation I found him very clear that the Islamist approach was about addressing the modern world, not trying to recreate the past. Hamas and Hezbollah also say that are not trying to recreate an old way of living, but are developing new ways of constructing social and economic models for their communities in the present world. From a Jacksonian point of view fundamentalism is not merely a form of regression with the release of functions from an earlier time or lower level of structure and complexity, but also most importantly incorporates an attempt at reconstruction from a position of dissolution. Given what Girard describes as the fundamental mechanism of mimesis (or non-conscious imitation) large-group identity regression may result in a reparative attempt to re-erect the boundaries that could obviate mimetic rivalry, but have been removed by the traumatic loss of or damage to large-group identity. It is as though the unsaid message from the frightened community is, 'We do exist; we are different and we may be acting in an aggressive (scapegoat) way, but it is in order to prevent worse (mimetic) violence'. This is of enormous importance because it makes clear that it is possible to identify within fundamentalism an innate reparative or reconstructive component, something that is often missed or dismissed by observers. Fundamentalism may in this way actually prevent some worse violence. It may not be impossible to relate to this component if it is recognized.

However, sometimes the emotion that leads to the regression is not just anxiety, but other emotions associated with humiliation, disrespect, and a sense of having been treated profoundly unfairly. The anxiety that these experiences generate about the expunging of one's identity and that of one's community is compounded by deep and abiding anger, hurt and a wish to attack and destroy, even if like Samson one brings down the temple on one's own head. It is not just an angry wish to attack an enemy but an overwhelming sense of justification in destruction because it is the right thing to do. In this context regression not only leads to a falling back into a form of thinking from the past, but to a way of thinking characterized by 'sacred values' that are not necessarily religious but transcend socio-economic metrics and also the complexities of difference between individuals. In this thinking 'I' am absolutely differentiated from 'the enemy other' and fused with 'my people'. My death is no longer the issue and my significance is only in the continued existence of my large group/culture.

The appearance of terrorism can, therefore, be re-interpreted not as mere criminal behaviour by individuals or groups and therefore, a moral issue (on either side) or as caused by mistaken and malign fundamentalist religious beliefs, but that both fundamentalism and terrorism are symptoms of temporo-spatial regression resulting from existential cultural threat and/or the experience of humiliation and injustice.

We are well aware as psychotherapists of the need from time to time for appropriate and sensitive containment (pharmacological, physical and social), if a patient with psychosis and their family are to be able to benefit from psychological therapies and find healing. By analogy we could make the proposition that the important role of security measures, containment and boundary-setting in the national and international context should not be portrayed as a moral intervention, but as being in the service of creating a context in which the disturbed thoughts, feelings and behaviour of the all the groups involved and the causes of the disturbance in relationships can be addressed.

If one puts these observations together, the increased disturbance may be interpreted as societal regression brought about by the fear of the loss, or in some cases the trauma of actual damage or loss, of large-group identity resulting from a combination of rapid socio-political changes in the past century. These might be summarized as follows – the advances in evolutionary science which remove the boundaries between humanity and the rest of the animal kingdom and introduce complexities of thinking which a majority of the population may find difficult to construe; the collapse of traditional authoritarian forms of government (monarchies, empires and tribal chieftains) with the advance of participatory democracy; the developments in information and communication technologies, greater speed and ease of travel and the borderless capacity for destruction in the nuclear age, all of which both excite interest and threaten large-group identity; the end of the Cold War, the collapse of communism and the widespread espousal of free market economics; in short the forces which we describe as rapid progress and globalization represent the loss of boundaries and our experience of time and space is shaken.

Religious fundamentalism is not merely ultra-conservatism and is an increasing phenomenon of all religious families of belief and some non-religious belief systems. It is not a reflection of individual personality types but can best be understood as a phenomenon of large-group psychology which occurs as a result of regression in the face of existential threat or trauma, and showing three related elements – the loss of some more developed social functions and complex ways of thinking, the return to or release of more elementary and rigid ways of thinking and being, and the reconstruction of the large-group identity from the remaining functions and faculties of the group. While described by its adherents in terms of eternal verities, it actually emerges in particular political contexts where there has been serious trauma and uncertainty, which bring out fear and aggression. While, it is also portrayed as being transcendent it frequently has direct and intentional political involvement. Fundamentalism is characterized by the diminution of individual freedom as individuals become fused with the group, and a concretizing of thinking and restrictions of behaviour, but its 'purpose' is to address the traumatic, frightening context with a reassuring clarity and definition and in this context there may be repair or reconstruction of the group identity which can help prevent further breakdown and this potentially positive component should not be disregarded. This phenomenon is sometimes thought to be a result of the persuasive teachings or propaganda of extreme thinkers, however, it seems to me that while this is a relevant contributor, it may better be understood as the self-regulating functioning of a complex social system.

Where there have been experiences of humiliation and deeply unfair treatment, and where it has not been possible to right these wrongs through peaceful democratic progress there may also be temporo-spatial regression and the sense of anxiety and existential threat is augmented by other emotions which result in the wish to attack and destroy. From regression in the context of this triad of features terrorism may emerge, and dealing successfully with it will require addressing the three core features.

From understanding to resolution

How can one address them? The question is often couched in terms such as, 'What was the key change that made Peace possible?' 'Who was the key individual who made the difference?' 'When did you know that the Process was irreversible?' While one can certainly give some answers to these questions, their linearity is misleading and complexity theories are more instructive.

As in Europe and South Africa, from which we learnt a great deal, so in Northern Ireland it was finally discovered that only a long process of containing difficult emotions, building inter-group relationships and untangling the historic repetitions of hurt and humiliation gave any hope for the future. It was remarkably similar to the process of individual and group psychotherapy; the systemic appreciation of family and group; the importance of creating an understanding of and motivation for analytic processes; the need for a long-term process of dialogue and the insistence that nothing and eventually no-one is excluded from having their say; the need for a reasonable and tolerable life circumstance; the skills of containment, interpretation and not allowing the process to become itself a resistance; setting down reasonable boundaries; containing the intolerable feelings; and behaving with respect.

Sustained political commitment over a long period of time whatever government was in power in Britain or Ireland was crucial. The Peace Process was a national, rather than merely a governing party commitment and so transcended electoral politics and considerations. The eventual inclusion of the representatives of all parties was the most difficult aspect, but as became apparent, it was the most necessary element and took years to achieve. Most political processes operate on the basis of excluding those you don't like or don't approve of, and avoiding the issues which are 'unacceptable'. The Irish Peace Process tried to be inclusive in every sense. The creation of sustainable economic development and cross-border trade created an external environment which was conducive, but contrary to what some analysts suggest, it was not the key factor which resolved the historic problem. The heart of the process was the deployment of patient, imaginative and skilful mediation through long-term Talks, and the long-suffering, accepting, analytic approach of the Talks Chairman, Senator George Mitchell was a model of the analytic psychotherapy posture. As in all good therapy there was also an element of institutional imagination and creativity and the embedding of international instruments of human rights protection ensured an ethical touchstone.

Rights, responsibilities and respect for minorities are difficult issues, but they cannot be avoided for they are at the core of the causes of many conflicts. The classic liberal commitment to freedom under the rule of law creates an environment for the protection of minorities, but even international legal norms and structures are rarely a sufficient guarantor for the partisans in a conflict. Usually particular political protections are required, at least for a transitional period because the level of trust between the various sides is so low.

Until people in any community embroiled in conflict give up the belief in violence as a means of solving their predicament they will not accept that the prize of peace is worth the price of peace. The community needs to be weary of war and prepared to accept an outcome which is less than their ideal – a compromise – for the sake of peace. Central to this is the rebuilding of the rule of law; the setting down of agreed boundaries to social behaviour. Demilitarization, decommissioning of illegal weapons, and reform of policing and the criminal justice system have been the most difficult and contentious issues of all in Northern Ireland, and the last to be resolved.

All of this takes a very great deal of time, not just because there are many issues and much history but because it takes time for communities to work through their feelings about the political changes, to modify expectations and deal with the very real pain of historic fears and grievances, as well as those which are much more recent in the life-times of all concerned. It is not just about getting leaders to reach agreement behind closed doors. It is about whole communities, led by their representatives, engaging in a process of change, and this means it has to be public and to take as long as it takes. People from stable societies often find the time required for this working through a deeply frustrating and depressing business – 'Why can't the leaders just forget about the past and get on with the job?' they say. As therapists, however, we are not only familiar with this experience, we also have some appreciation of why it is necessary.

Finally we must move beyond processes, formulae and regulations in preventing and resolving conflict. Whilst relationships, especially therapeutic relationships with individuals and communities cannot survive without the stability of structures and boundaries, they are based on more than the observance of rules and laws. There must also be a spirit of generosity and respect – what Freud meant I think when he talked of a treatment of love. Without this, the work cannot flourish and conflict is never truly put to the past. Boundaries, rules and rights can provide the context for internal and 'external' conflict to be stopped, but only a new culture of mutual respect can prevent it returning. Indeed, however, much we would like to believe that all cultures can simply find ways of getting on together without changing, cultural change is in fact necessary, if by 'culture' we understand ourselves to mean the way of 'being-in-the-world' of a community or large group. This cultural evolution is perhaps the ultimate challenge of a peace process.

The approach I have described requires a move away from the linearity that characterizes the current analysis where people are thought to adopt fundamentalist ideas, and then become politically radicalized and finally get involved in terrorism. Instead it puts in place a complexity model that sees these disturbed social relationships as systems affected by emotions resulting from existential anxiety leading to regression to more fundamentalist ways of thinking in the group. In the context of humiliation and injustice, we see the radicalizing of young people and when there is no peaceful democratic road to resolution there may be further regression into violent terrorism which is in no-one's real interest. This analysis also gives us clear indications of how we will need to act differently at a communal level, if we are to resolve these problems rather than deepen them. It is not just a question of how we manage others, but whether we in the West are prepared to change our own approach in order to have better and more peaceful international relationships.

Disclosure statement

No potential conflict of interest was reported by the author.

ORCID

John Lord Alderdice http://orcid.org/0000-0003-4322-0049

References

Ahmad, K. (2006) Great movements of the 20th century no 2, Jama'at- e-Islami. In *The Message* (pp. 1–8). New York, NY: Islamic Circle of North America.

Critchley, M., & Critchley, E. A. (1998). *John Hughlings Jackson father of English neurology*. Oxford: Oxford University Press.

Ey, H. (1962). Hughlings Jackson's principles and the organo-dynamic concept of psychiatry. *American Journal of Psychiatry, 118*, 673–682.

Erikson, E. (1956). The problem of ego identity. *Journal of the American Psychoanalytic Association, 4*, 56–121.

Freud, S. (1911). Formulations on the two principles of mental functioning. In J. Strachey (Ed.), *The standard edition of the complete psychological works of Sigmund Freud* (Vol. 12, pp. 215–226). London: Hogarth Press.

Gilligan, J. (1996). *Violence – our deadly epidemic and its causes*. New York, NY: GP Putnam's Sons.

Girard, R. (1977). *Violence and the sacred*. Baltimore, MD: The Johns Hopkins University Press.

Girard, R. (2005). Violence and religion. In Peter Walter (Ed.), *Das Gewaltpotential des Monotheismus und der Dreieine Gott* (pp. 180–190). Freibrug: Verlag Herder.

Jackson, J. H. (1887). Remarks on evolution and dissolution of the nervous system. *The British Journal of Psychiatry, 33*, 25–48. doi:10.1192/bjp.33.141.25

Volkan, V. (2006). *Killing in the name of identity*. Virginia, VA: Pitchstone.

Volkan, V. (2008). Religious fundamentalism and violence. In M. K. O'Neil & S. Akhtar (Eds.), *On Freud's 'The Future of an Illusion'* (Chap. 4, pp. 124–141). London: Karnac Books.

Whitehouse, H., Jong, J., Buhrmester, M. D., Gómez, Á., Bastian, B., Kavanagh, C. M., … Gavrilets, S. (2017). The evolution of extreme cooperation via shared dysphoric experiences. *Scientific Reports, 7*, 44292. Retrieved from http://www.nature.com/articles/srep44292.pdf.

Inflammatory projective identification in fundamentalist religious and economic terrorism

David Morgan

This paper contains the reflections and thoughts of the author, a psychoanalyst and consultant psychotherapist who through his work with violent patients at the Portman Clinic, and later as a specialist consultant with migrants, asylum seekers and political groups has developed some understanding of lone attackers and terrorist behaviour. He uses psychoanalytic theories such as inflammatory projective identification to understand how people can become inflamed through their experience of exploitation, economic and political hegemony, and loss of identity, so that they turn to violent evacuations into others. This violence toward the other is also reflected he says in western economic policy which has also been violent toward those who have been exploited through colonialism and more recently an unfettered market driven economy. This provides the drive to grievance and hate that can be so easily exploited by unscrupulous fundamentalist regimes.

Some reflections on projective identification

When I worked at the Portman Clinic, it was obvious that in some violent patients the pain and tedium of being a 'have not' from successive generations of 'have nots' meant that at some point, their powder keg of loveless emptiness and 'have notness' would explode into a drive to evacuate their experience into someone else.

This is well illustrated in a quote from Dr Murray Cox in discussion with Mark Rylance the actor, Cox a Consultant Psychotherapist at Broadmoor Hospital who on describing a murderous patient, used the phrase, 'I Needed a Life So I Took One' (Rylance, 2001, p. 5).This quote says it all; a profound failure to mourn because there is nothing good enough to allow the process to begin and leads to an enactment where loss is transferred – usually bodily – into another. A well-known case at the time was an erstwhile patient who had been denied admission, despite his desperate search for help, by many hospitals. When, at some point after all these negative responses to his need, he was refused a light for his cigarette by another man (who appeared to have everything this seriously ill man lacked), he attacked and killed him. Another well-known case at the time was of a young boy abducted and murdered by two other young boys many miles away from any help that might have intervened. It was clear (as I had some therapeutic involvement with the workers involved with the killers), that they too were psychically dying a long way from any help that might at some point have intervened with the underlying need to enact this horror – their internal horror – on the mind and body of another.

It is difficult not to think of these experiences now when writing this in the aftermath of the latest terrorist attack that occurred on Westminster Bridge, London, apparently by a so-called Jihadist, a loner, preyed upon through the internet by manipulative religious fundamentalists who hold a grievance, real or imagined (probably both), towards the West. This awful event ironically overshadowed the funeral of Martin McGuinness, the latterly successful Irish politician, formerly an ex-IRA commander and known euphemistically as the 'Butcher's Boy', not solely because his father was actually a butcher. McGuinness was allegedly responsible for both the death of Lord Mountbatten, but also two young innocent teenagers who were blown up with him and probably several other acts of terrorism on the British mainland.

Lone attackers

Lone attackers, like the recent Westminster terrorist are clearly manipulated and used to enact acts of terrorism for interested parties. These individuals are vulnerable men, often with some on-going history of violence, who are excited to overcome their internal disorders and discomforts through externalisation into others. They commit criminal acts and turn their backs on their families and culture, often leaving the UK or elsewhere for Isis and imminent death in holy Jihad or enacting terrorist atrocities and turning against the societies in which they live to murder and maim their fellow countrymen or others abroad. This so-called radicalisation is still increasing. The International Centre for the Study of Radicalisation at Kings College, London estimated that over 20,000 people from around the world moved to join what they saw as a holy war of Jihad, excited by highly subjective interpretations of ever-malleable religious scriptures.

They are different to the foot soldiers and bombers of some organisations such as the IRA, apparently motivated by political ideology and a wish to unite Ireland, although I would suggest that these IRA foot soldiers were again easy targets for leaders to use for terrorist ends, however justified those ends and means were felt to be. The religious fundamentalists offer 'pie in the sky' rewards for acts of terrorist atrocities, providing imagined heroic activities as a distraction from otherwise sad or isolated lives. Even genuine political liberation still attracts the zealot often driven to be used as a 'pawn in the game'.

As one young man I met in a migrant centre said, 'Growing up as a po' boy in Staines, working at a telephone call centre? Or becoming a Jihadist with a gun, 'a hero in my time', defending my brothers? No contest bruv!' Although it's worth noting that recently it has been disputed that the reward of the many virgins promised in contested religious writings is, in fact, a mis-translation, and should be read as raisins not virgins! – A disappointing outcome if ever there was one, even for the most enthusiastic dried fruit connoisseur!

The Jihadists are often deeply influenced by a simplistic ideology that aims to establish a caliphate, a return to religious fundamentalism; these religious beliefs that are, at this time, particularly threatened from the secular west and the infiltration of internet access and other technology. Is it just that religion is under threat and this is a retreat to certainty that these religious fundamental values offer, including the simplistic device of the infidel and unbeliever into whom all badness can be inflamed and projected?

The Welsh terrorist

On a more prosaic level and, closer to my own spiritual home, the depressed and violent young Welsh fire-setter that I saw at an NHS Clinic, affronted by my Welsh name and English accent, told me that the 'Sons of Glendower', a nationalist group dedicated to burning down second homes in North Wales, were the vanguard of a Welsh resurgence to rid his land, (and probably as he said mine) from the foreign invader. He had a point; his father's village had become a dormitory for holidaying wealthy people from Manchester to London who put little into the village and had caused the pub to go gastronomic, depriving locals of their traditional watering place – as in the song by the folk group 'Show of Hands' called 'Country Life':

> and the red brick cottage
> where i was born
> is the empty shell of a
> holiday home
> Most of the year there's no
> one there
> the village is dead and they
> don't care.
> Haven't been back since the
> pub closed down
> One man's family pays the
> price
> for another man's vision of
> Country life.
>
> "Country Life"
> Show of Hands

Loss of home

Every age has its hopes and fears and one can find individuals who feel threatened by the present and shun the world for the eternal promise of being reunited with some ideal. They harbour grievances and a dream of a return to some prelapsarian state, as in my Welsh fire-setter, of 'Welshness', mirroring the dream of a lost Eden, mirroring in a more extreme version, the lost caliphate that seems to motivate believers in the Middle East. We are in a profound period of economic crisis where the human industrial system could threaten to destroy all traces of tradition, certainty and belief, so this regression to a simplistic ideal is understandable.

Mechanisation, industrialisation, urbanisation and the massification of society takes precedence over religious and spiritual traditional values. We take the supremacy of modernity for granted; we can accept as a natural condition, what the Welsh philosopher Jones (1953 Lecture) called 'The crisis of lack of meaning'. But for some, these new forces threaten to destroy old value systems and they will behave as if their actual lives are under threat.

You can't defeat an ideology when it feels based on a justified grievance that their belief systems or actual home or homeland are under threat from the modern world and a wish to regress from the advances of modernity which seems to lack all spiritual awareness and religious observance, except that of materialism. As I heard one quasi fundamentalist say in a group for refugees, 'One episode of the Kardashians and I want to get my gun!' However, those of us not taken up with religious and fundamentalist views do not of course see any justification in taking the lives of others, or even attacking their properties, as a valid response to marginalisation, but it is at least an understandable knee-jerk response to the perception of cruel and thoughtless policies that have little awareness of local strife, and this sense of displacement and fear can be manipulated by the unscrupulous fundamentalist leader be it Bin Laden or indeed, at a less violent (for now) Donald Trump, and in the past Thatcher and Galtieri.

It may, as with my Welsh 'keep the home fires burning' compatriot, feel in a cruel changing world that can ride rough shod over cherished beliefs and traditions, that to resist that change is the only recourse. This is so clearly also a reflection of the individuals' struggle against their own repressive internal regimes that can only find relief through attacks on externalised representations, but to reduce all acts of rebellion and terrorism to this would be facile. It is important to understand the vulnerable lone wolf seeking an exciting method of evacuation of his mental strife into others or even the employed professional soldier doing the same thing at the bidding of their respective masters. However, collectively it may also begin to help us understand why we have become the legitimate target for terrorism.

Psychotic aspects of violence

At the moment, we in the West are in a period of communal violence that can be likened to the most difficult stages of psychotic illness, when the only response is one of containment and trying to minimise the damage. We are now the unwilling containers of these projectiles and we have to understand what we have been perceived to have done to deserve this (Vernon, 2015, p. 2). What is our valency in this? There appear to be two conflicting regimes at war with each other; religious fundamentalism in the form of a particularly virulent form of Islam, which most Muslims do not of course adhere to; the other an unfettered fundamentalist, Neo-liberal secular market economics that promulgates a vicious form of Social Darwinism; 'We are all revolutionary in our shopping habits now', that most of us don't want to adhere to, but unwittingly play a part in and until the arrival of climate change, refugees, soup kitchens, Brexit and Trump, could remain relatively unaware of. It was hard at the time not to feel that the horrific attack on the twin towers was also an assault on the symbol of this secular religion, of a 'winner takes all' culture, by a fundamentalist minority, who felt they had the right to enact murderous revenge for the perceived wrong-doings on the part of the West and specifically America.

So now, once safe democratic communities like ours are overtaken by enormous powerful feelings that can overwhelm our capacity to think clearly and act constructively, we are being projected into in a way that can lead to retaliation in kind. It is enormously attractive when evacuated into, to just evacuate back and retaliate. Like with the psychotic patient, what is being evacuated and relived and put into the body of the other are often experiences that represent the deepest traumas and these traumas can be dealt with through concrete retaliatory primitive evacuation – both by the terrorist and the economically disenfranchised and the victims of terrorism.

Inflammatory projective identification

We, at the moment, are the unwilling container for these explosive attacks and their aim, perhaps through the process of inflammatory projective identification, is to communicate fragmentation and psychosis into the minds and bodies of us the victims. 'As they pulled the trigger they looked into our eyes saying look at me, look at me' reported a victim at the Bata-clan Ballroom, Paris. The victim forced to face the unthinkable, the unthinkable parts of the perpetrator, which the perpetrator themselves cannot face within themselves, forces his victims to bear fragmentation and fear. Is it traumatic fragmentation that is being communicated, the threat to faith and fundamentalist thinking that is threatened with disintegration in the face of the apparent unlimited freedoms of secularism, with its liberal attitudes towards women and gay people and dogs and the dominance of materialism over spiritual and religious observation?

Ancient regimes

The old certainties offered by religious fundamentalism under siege from apparently godless thought and the dreaded horror of uncertainty that without religious or indeed, secular certainties (the Nazis and Stalin killed many more people than any religion has managed to do) that we have to live with. After all, the move from an external eternal authority (Allah, God, Jehovah, the Fatherland), to an internal conscience capable of self-regulation and morality is a road fraught with difficulty. This was something that the biblical entity Moses understood when, faced with his peoples' worship of the Golden Calf, drove him to concoct a superhuman being, who produced the commandments that we follow today, literally putting the fear of God into them. No doubt the golden calf worshippers who remained loyal to their own gods were seen as inferior. The wish always to regress to an ancient regime that offers absolute certainty and to have an infidel, non-believer, to carry all the uncertainty is profoundly seductive. In our own minor way, the regression to Brexit and little England and a 'Dad's Army' attitude is a similar albeit less violent search for certainty in an increasingly complex global economy.

Or is fundamentalist thinking more a violent response by beleaguered communities or people who feel under siege to the perceived unfettered aggression of western neoliberalism and it's God capital, which may include encroachments onto Islamic territories for purely strategic economic gain and the implicit support of despotic regimes providing little economic relief to the poor. Religion and nationalism always provide enormous succour to the hungry; nothing can really salve an empty stomach or deprivation like zealous hatred of another or a flag to stand under or a gun to put one's own fear sternly back into another. This is attractive not only at the threatened collective level, to reverse feelings of diminishment and loss, but also for the beleaguered individual frightened of his own mind, and having no other equipment to help manage insight, other than evacuating pain and horror into the other, usually someone perceived as privileged.

Trans-generational trauma

John Alderdice, a Consultant Psychotherapist and former speaker in the Northern Irish assembly agrees with the notion of trans-generational trauma going back many generations, particularly when that past is marked by hurt and abuse. The emotional impact in these situations of the past is felt as powerfully today in the present, especially when it has not been acknowledged or understood by anyone. Further, there are few past experiences that have more purchase on the present than those of humiliation. The desire for vengeance and the righting of wrongs can shape an entire life. They also have a particular power to generate violence because of the need to reverse the experience of humiliation that the aggressor is perceived to have inflicted. (Alderdice, 2005, p. 782).

A further insight in the victim/perpetrator dynamic is that victimhood often – not always – develops a sadomasochistic quality. The victim grows up in an environment in which the currency of communication is the exchange of pain. It is possible that no other currency of communication can be imagined. Hence, the dynamic can be perpetuated down the generations. Mark Vernon (2015, p. 2) says if we think we can appeal to rationality, such as 'why can't these people see reason?' we simply and fatally misunderstand what's going on. The outsider from a stable society regards the damage of communal violence as self-evidently not in the interests of either individuals or the society, and often they feel sure that people can be made to see sense. The insider understands that this view fails to appreciate the weakness of such rational argument in the face of profound violence. 'The terrorist has a profound need to make the perceived aggressor feel the humiliation that they felt'. This is like the patients I mentioned at the beginning who feel driven to evacuate pain, loss and humiliation into the other.

Socio-economic explanation

A different explanation has been put forward and that is a socio-economic one, in particular, the idea that terrorism has to do with poverty. To some extent it does; people who enact these attacks, the lone wolves, are often people at the lower end of the economic spiral. They feel resentful about their position and take refuge in a fundamentalist attitude, be it Islam, Christianity or nationalism and then feel justified in taking the lives of others, however collective. Terrorism often tends to arise in states that are on their way out of poverty. Bin Laden was a wealthy man. Alderdice (2005, p. 578) notes that things become vulnerable to violent breakdown, rather like when the depressed person gets better or begins to improve, they are often more likely to kill themselves. The tragic victims of terrorism are not the real targets; the victims are a way of getting at an authority, usually a government. In suicide bombing where the victim is, in part, the terrorist's own body, it also gets at the authority via the fear it generates.

Secondly, there is the need to understand the immense impact of the past, with all its emotion and meaning. Such emotions and meanings cannot simply be set aside. Alderdice (2005, p. 580) writes, 'The set of thoughts and feelings that has impressed me as most significant in generating violence has to do with experiences of disrespect and humiliation'. The desire to be treated with respect is 'insatiable'. As in the Hackney kids with guns and knives, joking when they have been dissed, what (Campbell, 2009) calls the reassertion of phallic dominance.

Psychoanalysis shows that, contrary to the popular view, time is often no healer. Grievances replace accumulated grief and it is here that terrorism can feed on identifications with past or historic victims and/or inner conflicts that the individual carries from the past. They feed a justification of righteous violence. 'The sense that the very existence of a community and all that it holds dear has been threatened, provokes deep fears and creates a capacity for responses at least as violent as those which it has experienced' (Alderdice Lecture, 2015).

An Ex-terrorist I saw said 'Joining a terrorist organisation was consciously seen both as a way of protecting their community and satisfying the wish for revenge for the death or injury or marginalisation of their loved ones'.

Terrorists may also be following rules that pertain more to the unconscious than conscious world; a dream world 'driven by basic feelings of hatred and rage or pleasure and elation; by uncomplicated associations that lack nuance and deploy sweeping symbolisms; by wish fulfilments; by a false sense of freedom from the strictures of waking reality, space and time'(Vernon, 2015, p. 2).

Alderdice suggests that describing terrorists as fundamentalists can be misguiding here. He prefers the word 'primitive' meant in the psychoanalytic sense, 'like that of a child who refuses to be comforted and screams out of sheer rage. More complicated still, the child may grow to enjoy its rage because it delivers a secondary gain; being able to control or even kill in fantasy the parent'. In this way, he suggests the terrorist derives a secondary gain where they can overcome feelings of impotence by being able to reverse these feelings through violent acts that command a great deal of attention. It reminds me of the arsonist who with a very small match can create such mayhem.

Further again, like parents who must contain the screams of their child and resist being drawn into its primitive world, governments and societies faced with terrorism must resist cultivating primitive feelings and actions in response. This begs the question what form containment can take other than suffering and hoping our intelligence agencies are able to prevent the worst atrocities (Vernon, 2015, p. 3).

Some violent responses are of course necessary. Alderdice (2015) states 'that whilst there may be the need at times to contain the terrorism with violence, violence that is presented as punishment or vengeance will not work. To put it another way, shoot-to-kill will not in itself deter. This is because of the need in terrorism to avenge perceived humiliations. So such actions by a strong government feeds the rage of the self-perceived weak, and further, makes the actions of the weak seem all the more honourable in the minds of those who share the humiliation'. He does say optimistically that 'a stage will arrive when it's possible to think more clearly and act constructively, and then everything must be on the table; be capable of being talked about. There must be no no-go areas'. This radical honesty and openness is said to lie behind the successes of the truth and reconciliation activities in South Africa, Northern Island and is lacking he says in the Middle East. Although I would argue this is more complex as I think our involvement in economic expansionism and exploitation of raw materials, specifically oil, in the Middle East has been utterly thoughtless and mendacious. The neglect of Palestinians by all western powers and the support for Zionist encroachment into disputed territories is an on-going horror. The identification with the aggressor within some of Israel's foreign policy seems unarguable as is the building of ghettos.

Appealing to long-term solutions is usually of limited help because emotion is the real issue. 'People who propose peace plans in such circumstances seem to be living with the unstated assumption that if the 'right plan' could be invented, everyone would suddenly grasp it with relief and implement it. Of course this is an illusion. It is not the content of a solution that is critical but the process of achieving it'. So the diagnosis of the problem is of limited use; it is the working through which is transformational. To put it another way, 'we must learn to tolerate the long, painful game and be prepared to invest accordingly when an opening, if it occurs, happens' (Alderdice, 2005, p. 781).

Unfortunately, we have not learned from Vernon, Alderdice and Northern Ireland. Instead of listening to the grievances arising from the Middle East, we in the West employ professional soldiers to perform what might seem acts of state sanctioned terrorism in the name of foreign policy, such as the invasion of Iraq, a peculiar response to the 9/11 attacks. In these situations, aren't those attracted to the armed forces, usually working class and relatively uneducated, whilst appearing to do their job to keep us safe from the extremists aggrieved at their perceived treatment by western policy-makers, also lay down their lives to enforce dubious policies of their countries (see US involvement in Vietnam, Soviet involvement in Afghanistan)? These young men volunteering to put themselves in a firing line are also arguably the victims of manipulation of distant senior political figures, driven more by economics than humanitarian concerns. Are they that different to the religiously motivated zealots of fundamentalist Islam? How many of us for instance would think it was worthwhile for anyone's sons or daughters to die in the service of keeping the Falklands Islands British or during the invasion of Iraq, whether this action is seen as an atrocity or 'liberation?' Even the relatively safe drone controller must suffer somewhere for his 'clean' and illegal tactical killings (Mayer, 2009, p. 71).

Western colonialism

The greatest acts of terrorism in the last century have in fact been perpetrated by western colonialism and economic expansionism. We are now arguably reaping the backlash of those policies. As Noam Chomsky (2017) in 'How to Create a Terrorist' on You Tube and Abby Martin (2017) in her recent work 'Empire Files' on You tube states, if you want to create a terrorist with legitimate grievances, look no further than US and UK foreign policy; they have been long-time supporters of brutal dictators in the Arab world and still are. We in the West have a long ignoble history of actually supporting extreme radical Jihadist Islamist states, as a barrier to foil Arab secular nationalism, which is what has been really feared. When these West sanctioned dictatorships fall, due to western invasion as in Iraq or the hopeful but ultimately sad Arab Spring, there is nothing substantial on the Left to take their place, as social democracy in these countries has not been encouraged by western foreign policy.

We have not been encouraging democratic nationalism in these states because it has not been in the interest of western economic and strategic policy to do so (Newman, 2006). When these puppet dictator regimes inevitably fall, there is no opposition to take their place except the fundamentalists with their return to ancient regimes and religious sharia law.

This example of aggression by the West is very familiar to us throughout the twentieth century. It was the same in Chile, with the repression and overthrow of the legitimate Allende government and the support of the brutal dictator Pinochet, and in many other theatres of foreign policy like Vietnam Nam and South Africa where local interests were repressed for the long-term economic or strategic interests of the West.

What was surprising in these coups and US sanctioned atrocities, is that there weren't more freedom fighters (or terrorists) from these countries to fight back. The treatment of Victor Jara, a singer and political activist in Chile, killed and tortured by the Pinochet regime, and the many, many who disappeared, demonstrates the effectiveness of US sanctioned terrorism in the part of the Pinochet government forces and their expertise with CIA assistance at eradicating any justified dissent.

This question of why isn't there more resistance against US hegemony is reminiscent of the same question asked of resistance to the Nazi regime. The answer is similar, in that the regime was brutal and all opposition crushed and destroyed; (see Sophie Scholl and the white cross).There were similar actions by US and UK governments in South Africa, in support of the Apartheid government against the ANC, the same in Pakistan where the most fundamentalist regime was supported and the most relevant in the current Jihadist problem, is the really shameful support of a truly hideous regime in Saudi Arabia that is known to finance virulent Islamic fundamentalism.

If you want to create a terrorist, ignore the effects of these policies on indigenous peoples and you create a legitimate grievance that can lead to acts of violence on western targets, effectively reversing the sense of helplessness, by evacuating it back into the perceived aggressor. For instance Nelson Mandela, was deemed a terrorist. He remained on the US terrorism list most of his life. Reagan and Thatcher both viewed Mandela as a threat. Indeed, he was at first involved in violent guerrilla actions against the apartheid state, although he was later openly regretful about this and Mandela is an interesting example of a 'terrorist', as he was able to change the way history thought about him and thus, change his legacy, as was in some ways, Martin McGuinness.

A terrorist in these situations is created, not born. We have to accept that no one has the right to take another's life, however, justified their grievances. However, it is true that some people can feel that their own identity, country and belief system is so under threat that the annihilation of the other, to preserve their own belief systems, is sometimes justified. In others, these same grievances can seem quite mad as in the uni-bomber in USA, but all, even the mad, are driven by a hostility to attacks on their beliefs, whether based on accurate perceptions of cruel regimes or imagined ones. This allows for a murderous response to the real or perceived attack as a threat to cherished beliefs, sometimes involving a regression to the ancient regime and old cherished ideas, as in religious fundamentalism, perhaps in the face of confusion and uncertainty, caused by the growing threat of secularism or loss of identity.

There can be an entrenchment in concrete thinking at these times because it provides a certainty that economic disadvantage or loss of power cannot. Poverty of various sorts can be alleviated by standing under a flag or proselytising a strict religion. The way to alleviate the seduction of these fundamentalist states of mind is to alleviate poverty and ignorance, to encourage an evolution to more symbolic forms, as a way out of dogma and flags, but this can only occur in situations that are conducive to thought or, as we might see it, towards a capacity to bear uncertainty and improvisation and flexibility. These usually occur in environments that have relative wealth and security.

How to create a terrorist

Therefore, to create a terrorist, this is what you do: firstly, ignore the underlying factors of poverty, inequality and western exploitation as well as the severe effects of climate change and global warming, arguably caused by unscrupulous western economic policies. This occurred in Syria where the effects of climate change pushed the rich farmers into cities after a 4 year drought. The rich class of farmers then created flash points and unrest in Aleppo where middle-class kids fall foul of police and then conflict ensues.

Secondly, ignore the creation of western influenced and financed dictators such as in the Middle East in countries set-up by Sykes and Picot after they carved up the Middle East along lines that don't take into account tribal loyalties. In these circumstances, brutal systems arose such as those of Saddam, Gadhafi and others. The USA recently, as we know for various reasons, moved into kick open doors in Iraq in a post-9/11 action, so that allegedly democracy would flourish. They de-Baathisised Iraq and the Baathist army who have war skills were then interned with Islamic fundamentalists and these old army types, disenfranchised Baathist military in prison then create an alliance with the fundamentalists.

So we are reaping the rewards of years of mismanagement or deliberate undermining of national democracy to maintain the status quo. This reminds us of the West's involvement in South Africa and the maintenance and support of the apartheid regime. In the case of Nelson Mandela, much of his terrorist identity came from his association with the African National Congress. The organisation remained a militant group long after Mandela had chosen a different path. It was in 2008, that the US delisted the ANC. So we have to understand that all terrorism may stem from a perceived justifiable cause for grievance and that however difficult it may be getting to this grievance and understanding it might be the beginning of some change. Nelson Mandela is an extraordinary example of a man who was able to do this at an individual level despite years of imprisonment and abuse. Martin McGuinness must have also achieved this to some extent.

This insight is hard to imagine with the like of Isis and their ilk. The attacks that they encourage probably do show that there has been a serious degeneration in the type of terror attacks that are no longer motivated by any ideological warfare but are now more the result of psychopathic rage. The lone terrorist, as at Westminster Bridge, will probably turn out to be a very ill man. The attacker in Russell Square in August 2016, was later admitted to Broadmoor Hospital with a diagnosis of paranoid schizophrenia. In previous histories of terrorism, the aim has usually been specifically a political one and as with the PLO and the IRA, the attacks were rational, however awful they might have been.

These current random attacks do seem to be carried out in the main by unstable young men for personal reasons and have nothing to do with politics or religion, except the idea of having a great enemy, does allow an externalisation of disturbing aspects of themselves into the other, thus, providing temporary relief from these disturbances. We have had other examples of this from other young men, who are not from an Islamic background, doing similar randomised acts, e.g. in America, in the form of James Jackson against black people; Dylan Roof on Afro-American Christians; Ali Sonboly on the American general public and gay people; and in this country Thomas Mair on an MP. I think these people are basically looking to evacuate parts of themselves that they find disturbing, the causes that they become wedded to, or are encouraged by, just provides them with the vehicle that they need to turn murderous thought into action.

In an unfair world

We must understand that in a world where there are disadvantages, neglect and unfairness, there will always be collective and individual activity to reverse the inferior position by finding other bodies and minds to carry it. One way of doing this is for the unstable individual, through their terrorist attacks, to project their impotence into the other. One aspect of this is to understand how feelings of impotence in the face of life's cruelties can lead to such retributive acts.

Maybe we can put into words the inchoate suffering that often remains unnoticed in pockets of the world that are unsung. To try and reach individuals who perpetrate the attacks, and also whole cultures that feel aggrieved by the perception that their lives, experience and belief systems are marginalised, we might yet save ourselves from the ever present threat of war and the evacuation into others that it perpetually offers. Instead of expansionism and the need for more growth to get bigger, maybe we just need to get better?

I would like to finish with a poem by a friend, a Congolese poet, JJ Bola (2015). He writes about state terrorism and the inhumanity of the effects of war on those that one knows or loves. This poem is set in Congo, but speaks to a suffering that is often unspoken and unknown and can lead to powerful pockets of resentment and rage over perceived aggression and loss. This is happening in many scenarios and they represent trans-generational time bombs of cruelty that can explode in some form at some time in the future. For instance, we create refugees by our economic policies and then we blame them for wanting a better life by coming to our country.

Tell them (they have names)
and when they turn the bodies over
to count the number of closed eyes.

And they tell you 800'000: you say no. that was my uncle.
He wore bright coloured shirts and pointy shoes.
2 million: you say no. That was my aunty.
Her laughter could sweep you up like
the wind to leaves on the ground.
6 million: you say no. That was my mother.
Her arms. The only place I have ever
not known fear.
3 million: you say no. that was my love.
We used to dance. Oh, how we used to dance.
Or 147: you say no. that was our hope. Our future. The brains of the family.
And when they tell you that you come from war: you say no. I come from hands held in prayer before we eat together.
When they tell you that you come from conflict: you say no. I come from sweat.
On skin. Glistening. From shining sun.
When they tell you that you come from genocide: you say no. I come from the first smile of a new born child. Tiny hands.
When they tell you that you come from rape: you say no. And you tell them about every time you have ever loved.
Tell them that you are from mother carrying you on her back. Until you could walk.
Until you could run. Until you could fly.
Tell them that you are from father holding you up to the night sky.
Full of stars. And saying look, child. This is what you are made of. From long summers. Full moons. Flowing rivers. Sand dunes.
You tell them that you are an ocean that no cup could ever hold.
JJ Bola
Poet

Disclosure statement

No potential conflict of interest was reported by the author.

References

Alderdice, J. L. (2005). Understanding terrorism: The inner world and the wider world. *British Journal of Psychotherapy, 21*, 577–587.

Alderdice, J. L. (2015). *Devoted actors the psychology of fundamentalism*. Public lecture political mind seminars. British Psychoanalytic Society, London.

Bola, J. J. (2015). Word. *Amazon*. 8–9.

Campbell, D. (2009). *Gangs, guns and the absent father*. MLPC Lecture.

Chomsky, N. (2017). YouTube 9/2/2015.

Martin, A. (2017). Empire files. YouTube.

Mayer, J. (2009, October 26). The predator war. *New Yorker Magazine*, pp. 24–32.

Newman, R. (2006). YouTube.

Rylance, M. (2001). Q&A: 'Mark Rylance discusses Richard III and his long interest in mental health issues.' Retrieved from https://www.psychoanalysis-bpa.org/docs 5-6

Vernon, M. (2015). *Paris, terrorism and psychoanalysis*. Retrieved from http://www.markvernon.com/paris-terrorism-and-psychoanalysis

Rage and hatred in infants: conditions which facilitate development versus those which result in tragic delays or alarming distortions

Anne Alvarez

The paper traces some possible trajectories of aggressive behaviour in children and adolescents. It distinguishes three contributing factors: 1. Disturbance or Disorder; 2. Deficit and Neglect; and 3. Deviance. Therapeutic technique may need adjusting depending on which factor is dominant at any moment. Two dimensions which seem to run through these categories are first, the question of which type of violence is occurring - that is, the motivation and emotion which accompany the violence; the second question is whose violence: that is, when we study the inner world of aggressive children we discover vast differences in the relationships between the self and the internal objects or representational figures of other people. These two questions will be raised whenever we try to treat these children or adolescents.

Introduction

In this paper, I discuss some distinctions about different kinds of violence and motives for violence stemming from my experience working with very violent children and their psychopathology. In no way, of course, can I say there are likely to be exact correspondences with the childhood development of radicalized adults. However, they may represent possible trajectories of abnormal development which lead to the expression of different types of and motivations for violence in adulthood.

I distinguish three factors contributing to violent behaviour: (1) Disturbance, (2) Deviance and (3) Deficit and neglect. In addition to the question about what different types of motivation for violence exist, there is also a second question about whose violence it is, that is, when we study the inner world of violent children we discover vast differences in the relationships between the self and the internal objects or representational figures of other people.

An earlier version of this paper was first published in: Williams, Paul (Ed.) (2011). *Aggression: From Fantasy to Action*. Karnac, London.

Which violence? The distinction between disturbance and deviance

Meloy, a psychologist who has had a long and intensive experience assessing violent inmates in prisons in the San Diego area in California, has made a very helpful distinction between what he called 'affectively evoked aggression' – i.e. 'hot' aggression evoked by the perception of threat versus 'predatory aggression' which is directed towards the destruction of prey, usually for food-gathering in sub-human species (Meloy, 1996). This latter type of violence involves minimal autonomic arousal and vocalization. Meloy gave a helpful example illustrating these two types of violence. 'When a household cat is cornered and threatened, the neurochemical set produces a display of affective aggression: hissing, hair standing on end, dilating pupils, active clawing arching back. When the same cat is stalking a bird in the back-yard, predatory aggression dominates: quiet stalking of the prey, the absence of ritualistic display, and focussed attention on the target.' (Meloy, 1996, p. 25) He thought that the type of disturbed offenders who exhibited affective aggression were more likely to be borderline-type personalities following Kernberg's (1984) levels of personality organization or, I would add borderline psychotic, whereas the predatory type of aggression was the hallmark of the psychopath. Meloy suggested that the anecdotal descriptions by workers in forensic treatment and custody settings of certain patients' or inmates' eyes as 'cold, staring, harsh, empty, vacant, and absent of feeling' (Meloy, 1996, p. 74) and the consequent feeling of eerie fear should be taken very seriously. It is especially chilling to experience this with a young child. Meloy points out that this experience of chilling fear does not seem to arise with even very dangerous explosive combative patients who are more likely to use the affective type of violence.

We need more study of the trajectory of the development of psychopathic aggression, that is, of the conditions under which hot aggression turns cold. Addictive violence may have begun as a defence against some horror, then gradually acquired sadistic and exciting overtones, but eventually, under certain conditions of lifelong chronicity, become almost motiveless and certainly casual. The enormity of the act may no longer bear any relation to the amount of feeling left in the perpetrator. An addiction is different from a defence. Here, it is pertinent to distinguish between anger, rage and bitter hatred. Most babies and young children may be capable of feeling rage and fury when frustrated, and those who are abused and neglected, if they have enough fight left in them, may feel such feelings all the time. They may feel like killing someone, and Melanie Klein was clear that this wish was in all of us at times (Klein, 1946/1975). While some violent acts have a more purely evacuative motive – to get the aggression out on anyone anywhere – others do, I believe, carry a powerful intention to kill. Somewhere in our brains, bones, teeth and nails, I think we can know, even as children, what it is to want to kill, and to mean to kill – finally and forever. These feelings are not the province only of the psychopaths but they are hot, not cold.

I think, however, that real hatred probably takes a while to develop. Hatred is a more abiding, lasting feeling than anger or rage, and probably requires a more organized personality and a well-developed sense of the existence of other people in the internal world. It needs some degree of object constancy, probably capable of being embedded in the personality in the second year of life. I have seen two children, both aged three, who were full of hatred and already had cold hardened psychopathic qualities. Both were a great danger to their younger siblings. One, a little boy, had been raised by a mother who hated him, and the other, a little girl, in a Romanian orphanage. There is also the problem, which may be particularly relevant to the current topic, which is the deadly combination of a borderline paranoid personality with psychopathy. I can think of one 12-year-old boy, Georgio, who lived in a large Mediterranean city, who could get into almost delusional persecutory states about his parents and some of his schoolmates whom he often attacked. At the early stage of his treatment, he consistently drew the most horrific scenes of torture, often carried out by a monstrous being who always had one arm amputated. Gilligan writes about psychopathic murderers who claim that they have felt dead and that they died inside a long time ago (Gilligan, 2016). Georgio's therapist and I used to wonder if this boy felt deeply castrated at the centre of his being. His frequent attacks on his parents were sometimes carried out in a rage, but at other times, in a very planned and calculated manner. The intact bit of his personality could use his paranoia in very effective ways. He was also extremely arrogant and his omnipotence hid a deep sense of buried shame. His parents appeared to be loving and concerned but he did once say he remembered his mother force-feeding him when he was still in his highchair. I shall return to the issue of control and lack of control later. After a while and some family treatment at home alongside the therapy, Georgio's pictures changed: the monster was chained in the basement and there was a sort of bleak uneasy peace above and in the town outside the dwelling place. But a year later, some decent trustworthy figures and a better world began to appear. He had talked a lot about evil in the world and the world being evil, and perhaps the overwhelming nature of some hatred can only be expressed and captured through a vision as vast as the kind of apocalyptic fundamentalism we are witnessing today.

Whose violence and a return to the question of which violence

I would like to distinguish three factors which may need to be identified in acts of violence: disorder, deviance and deficit All of these concern the relation between the self and its internal objects in the inner world. I will look at the location or source of the anger, in the sense of whether, within the patient's inner world, it is felt to arise from the self or from the inner representational figures.

Factor 1: disturbance or disorder

(a) *Aggression arising within the self as a reaction towards a figure felt to be infuriatingly frustrating or disappointing, or else highly dangerous and terrifying.* I am talking here about a paranoid reaction where there is considerable persecutory feeling, similar to Meloy's affectively evoked aggression. In some cases of abuse, trauma or persecution, there may be a profound and lasting sense of outrage and injustice. One child whom I treated had been horribly abused by his mentally ill mother, and during a long break in treatment when I stopped to have a baby, took to killing small animals in the fields near his home. He had also been attacking anything soft or vulnerable in my playroom. For a long while, I interpreted his jealousy of my baby, until an analyst called Sydney Klein pointed out that I was persecuting him with my interpretations, and I began to talk about, instead of jealousy, a feeling of betrayal. This more sympathetic understanding turned things around quite quickly and led me – eventually and ever since – to want to understand more about the sense of rightful needs, such as the need for justice and even for fantasies of revenge (Alvarez, 2012). The novelist Milan Kundera (1982) pointed out that these can lead to necessary 'rectifications', and, I would add that, for victims of torture or injustice, these fantasies may be a necessary step on the way to some degree of healing. I have had to learn that if you just keep telling the person how angry he is, you may overwhelm him with more of his already intolerable helpless rage. If, on the other hand, you understand that sometimes badness needs to stay out there, you can talk about his feeling, not that he wished you hadn't gone off to have a baby, but that he feels you shouldn't have done so. They and you therefore deserve punishment. I imagine many terrorists feel they are engaged in acts of rectification – putting things right, but not by acts of reparation, which would imply love and guilt.

(b) *Aggression which is not the patient's own, but erupts because he is possessed by a violent figure which has been internalized or identified with unconsciously.* This can occur in post traumatic stress disorder. It acts like a 'foreign body' (Williams, 1997). He may have witnessed much violence, or received it, and may even be in unconscious identification with the aggressor, but my point is that the identification is unconscious, and the child may not know why he did something or where the impulse came from (perhaps when Jon Venables and Robert Thompson, the killers of Jamie Bulger,[1] each accused the other of throwing the first stone, they meant it.) Many borderline psychotic people do not feel as though it was themselves carrying out the violent act. They may be right, in a sense, if there was a considerable degree of depersonalization and dissociation. Here, we need to show the patient that we understand that 'it is in them to do' but not say things such as, 'You were very angry when you ...' because sometimes he was not angry, although someone inhabiting him inside certainly was. He felt possessed, not angry.

(c) *Aggression arising when a child has been very heavily projected into by a caregiver who sees him as violent when in fact he is not.* The child begins to identify with the figure's view of him and cannot shake it off. Here, a fairly non-violent child is seen as violent by a possibly quite paranoid caregiver. I have seen this situation where the child may begin to act in a violent manner, but the observer may begin to get a sense that when the violence erupts, it is not really him doing it. One 3-year old boy, Kenneth, was really believed by his very paranoid mother to be evil. She believed he had been out to destroy her peace of mind ever since he was a baby. Although by age 4 he often was aggressive, his very sensitive therapist, and also a very kind teacher, could both get him out of these states by telling him, in their different ways, that they could see that he didn't mean it (this would be a very foolish thing to say to a psychopathic child, who, by the time he has hardened up, has owned it). The therapist also had to make it clear to Kenneth over and over again that she neither expected nor wanted violence from him. Unfortunately, he had to change to less understanding, somewhat more critical and over-reactive teachers, and, in addition, his therapy had to be interrupted for a period. The next therapist who took him on at age 6 noticed that he had begun to identify with this violent identity – he had begun to own it. He presumably had had to make some sense of what he was being exposed to, and perhaps in a terrible way it stopped him going mad with confusion. This can signal a dangerous progress towards the deviance which I have touched on earlier and will elaborate below: there are points in development where regularly occurring states of mind become personality traits (Perry, 1995).

Factor 2: violence and aggression owned, idealized and eventually found to be thrilling

(a) *Aggression arising where the child has begun to own the identification with the aggressor.* This develops in psychopathic patients, or with paranoid ones. In the case of the psychopathic children, the internal object is not seen as dangerous, simply another piece of prey. These children may be suspicious, but they are not angry and they are not afraid. People are afraid of giants, but only suspicious of pygmies or equals.

(b) *Addiction to violence.* Violence has become habitual, as any of the above factors combine and lead to secondary developments. A consequence of such addiction is that it may become a solution to much more minor problems and more minor stresses. However, if there is a reactivity to particular forms of stress, sensitivity on the part of residential workers, therapists and families to current or recent separations, changes, losses, may help to turn the apparently invisible and seemingly minor triggering stimuli into visible, verbalizable and thinkable-about issues. That aspect however, is sometimes easier to deal with than the casually habitual aggression.

(c) *Perverse excitement accompanying violence.* This is a worrying development, particularly as ordinary pubertal sexuality may be blocked because of personality difficulties. Grotstein points out, in the introduction to Meloy's book *The Psychopathic Mind: Origin, Dynamics, Treatment* (Meloy, 1996), that psychopaths experience a characteristic hypo-reactivity of their peripheral autonomic nervous system and pursue exciting aggression to compensate. One patient I heard of recently who is fascinated by hate preachers, can get quite sexually excited when he talks about others viewing Isis videos of beheadings. He also has a voyeuristic sexual perversion and has been investigated by the police for both preoccupations.

Factor 3. Deficit and neglect: deficits in the development of loving affectionate relations between the self and other people, in self-reflective function, and in the capacity for ordinary excitements and pleasures; the issue of neglect and the issue of shame, pride and agency

(a) *Deficit in the internal representation of good figures and of a good self, and of intelligent figures.* This produces hopelessness, despair and sometimes emptiness and eventual deep cynicism. Many abused and traumatized children are not simply abused and traumatized: they are usually deprived as well of ordinary opportunities for pleasurable interactions, the stimulation of learning and of ordinary interpersonal relations – the neglect of neglect (Music, 2009). Here, I want to say something about the importance of `stupid' objects. I have seen too often the murderousness of certain children not towards their abusive fathers, who may have been quite lively in between episodes of violence, but towards the depressed or denying mother who is seen as weak and unable, as it were, to get it. This sometimes evokes more rage than the actual abuses of the tormentor. I think the `stupid object' requires much more study. The image of all adults, or all women, say as being stupid may not be the result of the ordinary adolescent contemptuous devaluing – it may be the result of never having found a parent interesting or worth listening to or looking up to. This sometimes occurs where there are depressed, preoccupied or drug addicted parents. Such figures may be unvalued, not devalued and they may evoke huge rage and despair. A factor that can feed outrage and violence is the feeling that nobody out there 'gets it' and this can arise in infancy where there is insufficient experience of the sense of agency or efficacy, that is, the capacity to make an impact on someone. Success can lead to pride and self-respect, failure can lead to despair and shame.

(b) *The missing Factor: Agency, contingency and timing: An intersubjective experience.*

The normal infant is, in many ways, helpless and dependent; but he is also competent, thoughtful, alert, and, when conditions allow, full of passionate curiosity about his world. Developmental researchers have spent decades now in attempting to analyse the separate elements in the conditions essential for healthy cognitive/emotional development. The sense of efficacy – or agency – is one such element identified by Broucek (1979). He has suggested that what he has called the 'sense of efficacy' – and the pleasure associated with it – are the foundations of self-feeling. In his book, Broucek (1991) cites Jonas (1974), who thinks that the source of the concept of causality is in the experience of the body exerting itself in action. Broucek (1991, p. 28) also describes Tomkins (1981) observation that infants, soon after birth, replace reflex sucking with voluntary sucking and reflex visual tracking with voluntary visual tracking. Broucek points out that Tompkins insists that from the first moments of life infants are engaged in making good scenes better by *doing it themselves.* Broucek thinks this is one of the first manifestations of intent and of the will – a fascinating theory on the origins of basic self-feeling. Yet Broucek is clear that the infant is usually acting on someone and we might need to add, therefore, the equal importance of OBJECT-feeling – that is, feelings about the nature of the human beings or – in the language of attachment researchers – internalized representational figures upon which the baby sees himself acting. Clearly, causal experiences are not purely physical; they are also mental. The ordinary baby has plenty of experiences of his mind exerting itself in action and producing effects on another mind. There may be more, by the way, to the sense of agency than pure power or mastery, even though this latter element may not be negligible. I do not think this can any more be understood simply in terms of 'infantile omnipotence' (Klein, 1946, p.7) or of Winnicott's (1945) 'illusion' – babies may be helpless physically, but they are anything but helpless emotionally and socially – that is, if the caregivers allow them to be. Reddy has shown from the early months of life on, babies like to tease and get a laugh (Reddy, 2008).

A very interesting study shows how important is the sense of agency to infants; it also shows that the type and sophistication of the 'defences' available to the infant when this is disappointed seem to depend on his age and stage of emotional and cognitive development. In a 1979 paper Broucek reviewed a number of research studies on 'contingency'. He described the baby's joyful delight in discovering that he himself can be a causal agent of events. The infant shows much pleasure – smiling, excitement and cooing – at the discovery that there is a contingent relationship between his own initially spontaneous behaviour and an event in the external world and 'the subsequent ability to produce *at will* the external event through repetition of the antecedent act'. (Broucek, 1979, p. 312.) The conclusion seems inescapable that the infant's pleasure in this situation is pleasure in being the cause'. He stressed the importance of the will – a relatively unexplored subject in psychology and in psychoanalysis and described what happens when babies are denied adequate opportunities for the experience of efficacy: if the baby is very young, the capacity for initiative may atrophy. Papousek and Papousek (1975), in a laboratory experiment, first gave babies the opportunity to cause an event to take place. The babies' pleasure was, apparently, insatiable. The experiment showed that there was nothing special about the event itself that was rewarding – it was the ability to make it happen that mattered to the babies. The experimenters then deprived the babies of this satisfaction, and found that the first reactions were intensified respiration, pulse rate and perspiration. However, an even more worrying situation arose: some of the babies began to 'play possum'; they lay motionless with non-converging, staring eyes and sleep-like respiration. Papousek and Papousek suggested that this passive state of a sort of 'total inner separation from the environment' was more likely to appear in babies under two months of age; infants older than three months placed in similarly frustrating situations seemed more able actively to avoid everything connected with the unsolvable problem. Active avoidance and passive unresponsiveness were thus seen as very different ways of reacting to a feeling of inefficacy; the result in both cases was a lowering of attention and orientation. There may be some interesting issues here for diagnostic and clinical consideration. Clinicians have considered it sometimes to be an achievement and a development when the unresponsiveness of an autistic child or a neglected child changes from being more automatic and helpless to being more actively intentional, when, for example, dull eyes are replaced by a deliberately averted gaze (Alvarez, 1992, p. 98; Reid, 1989, Personal communication). There are cognitive and object-relational effects where this sense of agency is lacking, where the universe is not felt to be modifiable, and where there is severe lack of contingency. This can lead to profound feelings of impotence and inadequacy.

Conclusion

I have tried to give some idea of the importance of distinguishing types of violence and sources of violence within the internal world of object relationships. I distinguish three factors contributing to violent behaviour: disturbance, deviance and deficit/neglect. I identify three types of disturbance – aggression towards an object felt to be bad and persecutory, aggression arising from possession by or identification with, a violent object, and aggression due to an internalization of an object which views the self as violent even where it is not. I also sketch a deviance trajectory from habitualness, through to addiction, on to perverse excitements. I then discuss two factors involving deficit, that of deficit in the internalization of good objects, and another concerning deficits in the sense of agency. This should be regarded as only work in progress, and although it may be a start towards refining and developing our diagnostic and therapeutic instruments, it is unlikely to mean that the therapeutic work with very disturbed aggressive patients is ever going to be easy.

Disclosure statement

No potential conflict of interest was reported by the author.

Note

1. James Bulger was a 2-year-old boy from Merseyside, UK, who was murdered in 1993. He was abducted, tortured and murdered by two 10-year-old boys, Robert Thompson and Jon Venables. Both boys were subsequently found to have suffered abuse themselves.

References

Alvarez, A. (1992). *Live company: Psychoanalytic psychotherapy with autistic, borderline, deprived and abused children.* London and New York, NY: Routledge.

Alvarez, A. (2012). *The thinking heart: Three levels of psychoanalytic therapy with disturbed children.* London: Routledge.

Broucek, F. J. (1979). Efficacy in infancy: A review of some experimental studies and their possible implications for clinical theory. *International Journal of Psychoanalysis, 60*, 311–316.

Broucek, F. J. (1991). *Shame and the Self.* London: Guilford Press.

Gilligan, J. (2016). Can psychoanalysis help us to understand the causes and prevention of violence? *Psychoanalytic Psychotherapy, 30*, 125–137.

Jonas, H. (1974). *Philosophical essays.* New York, NY: Prentice-Hall.

Kernberg, O. F. (1984). *Severe personality disorders.* London: Yale University Press.

Klein, M. (1946/1975). Notes on some schizoid mechanisms. In *The writings of Melanie Klein, vol III Melanie Klein: Envy and gratitude and other works.* London: Hogarth.

Kundera, M. (1982). *The joke.* Harmondsworth: Penguin.

Meloy, J. R. (1996). *The psychopathic mind: Origin, dynamics, treatment.* London: Jason Aronson.

Music, G. (2009). Neglecting neglect: Some thoughts about children who have lacked good input, and are 'undrawn' and 'unenjoyed'. *Journal of Child Psychotherapy, 35*, 142–156.

Papousek, H., & Papousek, M. (1975). *Cognitive aspects of pre-verbal social interaction between human infants and adults.* Parent Infant Interaction, CIBA Foundation symposium, No. 33, Elsevier, Amsterdam.

Perry, B. (1995). Childhood trauma, the neurobiology of adaptation and "use-dependent" development of the brain: How "states" become "traits". *Infant Mental Health Journal, 16*, 271–291.

Reddy, V. (2008). Feeling shy and showing off: Self-conscious emotions must regulate self-awareness. In J. Nadel & D. Muir (Eds.), *Emotional development* (pp. 136–139). Oxford: Oxford University Press.

Tomkins, S. (1981). The quest for primary motives: Biography and autobiography of an idea. *Journal of Personality and Social Psychology, 41*, 306–329.

Williams, G. (1997). On introjective processes: The hypothesis of an omega function. In *Internal landscapes and foreign bodies: Eating disorders and other pathologies* (p. 97). London: Duckworth.

Winnicott, D. W. (1945). Primitive emotional development. In *Collected papers* (pp. 145–156). London: Hogarth.

Terror, fundamentalism, and male adolescence

Elisabeth Rohr

Terror and fundamentalism have received considerable attention within the scientific community in the last decade. But what is missing is an interdisciplinary, mainly psycho-social study that links terror and fundamentalism with male adolescent developments. In this paper, it is argued that fundamentalism is a necessary, maybe even essential basis for terrorism, but that terror almost always is connected with young male actors and their pathological adolescent biographies. Exploring this connection between terror, fundamentalism and specific pathological developments in male adolescence opens up new perspectives of understanding terrorism. Adolescence in general has been considered a phase of severe identity crisis, extensively studied and investigated in psychoanalytic theory. It seems that specific psycho-social and religious conditions and individual dispositions can turn a young male adolescent into a terrorist. In this sense male adolescent identity crisis seems a risk factor for terrorism.

Introduction

It is not an easy task to write about terror and fundamentalism. Both topics deserve in itself special and detailed attention. Myriads of scientific investigations dealing both with terrorism and fundamentalism, especially since 9/11, demonstrate quite convincingly that this challenge has been met by the scientific community, even on a global scale (Armstrong, 2000; Beier, 2006; Pratt, 2017).

However, if you want to study the conjunction and the linkage between terror and fundamentalism the task turns out to be quite a different challenge, especially if you consider male adolescence. Reviewing the extensive literature on the above mentioned subjects, it is surprising to find out, that almost all of the terrorists – with few exceptions – were men and in the majority, young men. But this obvious manifestation of gendered aspects surrounding terror has hardly gained any major attention in international studies about terror and fundamentalism. Although this fact is often mentioned, it is mentioned 'en passant', without focusing on it and without using it as an exciting and promising starting point for further investigations. The few psychoanalytic orientated studies that take this eye-catching fact of male dominance surrounding terror and also religious fundamentalism seriously usually focus all attention on early childhood development and subsequent disturbances (Beier, 2006; Stein, 2009; Summers, 2006). What is ignored and subsequently left out of all considerations is the specific development and theoretical reflection about male adolescence and post-adolescence. Yet, psychoanalytic investigations have shown that this period of life is decisive for the formation of gendered and adult identities (Blos, 1979; Laufer, 1965). Moreover, research has suggested that psychic modifications in this phase can in many cases rehabilitate early childhood experiences and even straighten out childhood deformations to a certain extent (Leuzinger-Bohleber & Lebiger-Vogel, 2016). When talking about male actors of terrorism and about a male dominated agency within fundamentalist communities, we necessarily have to take into account male developments in adolescence. That led me to concentrate on this missing link within the theoretical frame of understandings concerning terrorism and fundamentalism. It was also the opportunity to introduce a psychoanalytic perspective. On this basis, I would like to propose that terrorism in conjunction with fundamentalism is not only and not exclusively determined by political and religious reasons, but that it is linked with unresolved conflicts and specific and psychopathological processes during male adolescence. I would like to therefore suggest an understanding of terror and fundamentalism that includes psychological dimensions, and pose the question: Is terror in conjunction with fundamentalism perhaps the result of a unilateral, desperate as well as distorted and alienated resolution of a severe and unresolvable male adolescent crisis?

The scientific base of my arguments

In the course of the following reflections, I would like to offer three different threads to argue and to consolidate the above outlined thesis.

First, I would like to review Kepel's (1993) arguments concerning religious fundamentalism (or revivals) laid down in his book: *The Revenge of God. The Resurgence of Islam, Christianity, and Judaism in the Modern World.*

Kepel (1993) argues that all of these movements – even though they flourish in quite different religious communities – resist the spirit of modernity and secularism, and this resistance is the common denominator for virtually all fundamentalist movements. Nevertheless, he insists, they cannot be dismissed simply as a mere reaction and antithesis to modernity.

He further points out that the simultaneity of these fundamentalist revivals is not coincidental, but that they are reflections of widespread and profound discontent with modern ways of life and modern society. At the same time he asserts that over-reductionist accounts of fundamentalism that see it exclusively as a reaction to modernity and secularism are not an adequate description of the complexity of the problem. Fundamentalism is more than a mere reaction and an antithesis to modernism and secular life.

Secondly, I would like to present and discuss the main arguments of Martin Riesebrodt (1993), to be found in his book: *Pious Passion: The Emergence of Modern Fundamentalism in the United States and Iran.* Interestingly, the direct translation of his book, originally written in German, is more telling and the title of the book reveals his core thesis: 'Fundamentalism as a patriarchal protest movement' (1990). Focusing on underlying gender issues within the North American evangelical and the Iranian Muslim fundamentalist and revival movements, Riesebrodt is able to touch on issues that are essential for the understanding of fundamentalism, thus broadening common explanations that usually leave out any gender specific analysis. His book is convincing, as he is able to show that there are similar structures, anxieties and desires found in evangelical and Muslim fundamentalism that seem to end up in a similar diagnosis to explain their view and understanding of the world's misery. They come to similar conclusions to solve their problems and in some cases even similar forms of action.

Finally, I would like to use the findings in these above mentioned studies to connect them to theories of psychoanalytic understanding of adolescence, focusing especially on male adolescent development. I rely on the studies of Bohleber (1992) and Leuzinger-Bohleber and Lebiger-Vogel (2016) and on Csef (2017), who clarify and analyze the psychological reasons behind the radicalization of young male adolescents and their refuge into Jihad warriors.

Defining terrorism and fundamentalism

To further discuss scientific studies about terror and fundamentalism it is necessary to clarify what is to be understood by the terms 'terrorism' and 'fundamentalism'.

'Definitions of terrorism are legion' writes Pratt (2017, p. 438) and then continues to offer a first definition of 'terrorism': 'Intimidating the innocent as a modality of action is perhaps one general characteristic, as is the fact that, for the most part, terrorism involves violent behaviors undertaken for political and/or ideological purposes. Terrorism may be regarded as comprising a complex of criminality, psychology, and ideology: there is no single or simple definition or analysis' (Pratt, 2017, p. 438). What is convincing about this definition is the fact that it clearly links terrorism with religion and with psychology, pointing out at the same time that 'terrorism is a multi-faceted phenomenon' (Pratt, 2017, p. 439). It is important to acknowledge that terror almost always has a religious or at least an ideological foundation that is based on fundamentalist beliefs, but that it needs additionally psychology to really understand the phenomenon.

Now fundamentalism: How can it be defined and what do we have to understand, when we use this term? Again Pratt delivers a very sound explanation and definition. He writes: 'For nearly a century the term "fundamentalism" has referred to a set of specific Christian beliefs and an allied ultra-conservative attitude' (Pratt, 2017, p. 440). This does not mean however that fundamentalism did not exist before or outside Christianity, but the term 'fundamentalism' was first created and used in a Christian context. Since then 'the use of the term has broadened: the term 'fundamentalism' more or less names a religio-political perspective found in many if not all major religions in the contemporary world' (Pratt, 2017, p. 440).

Pratt then continues and points out that 'fundamentalism arose in a uniquely Christian context; it has since migrated into other arenas of discourse' (Pratt, 2017, p. 440) – for example, into political debates, describing rigid, stern, splitting and polarizing attitudes. Common to all these different fundamentalist arenas of discourse is the understanding that there is a non-negotiable set of doctrines that do not allow any interpretation or changes by anyone. To this non-negotiable set within traditional Christian conviction belongs the rejection of Darwin's evolutionary theory and the conviction that the bible has to be understood literally, because it contains God's own word and for that reason each single word is holy and non-alterable. 'Fundamentalism is the justification of a belief system on the basis of an illusory literal interpretation of a text claimed to be infallible' (Summers, 2006, p. 334). This is also the basic and common ground for Jewish and Muslim fundamentalism and for that reason also the basis for any political or ideological fundamentalism defending books or texts that are considered sacrosanct.

In contrast to Pratt's more general definition Beier (2006) understands the rise of fundamentalism as a mostly male expression of protest and of rage about 'a fundamental sense of having his right to exist questioned' (Beier, 2006, p. 303). It is as such an expression of a severe conflict and even identity crisis 'when orthodox people began to organize for survival in a world dominated by the non-orthodox' (Beier, 2006, p. 303). This feeling of having one's own existence questioned might lead 'to a militant attempt to assure oneself that one matters' (Beier, 2006, p. 303). Male protest and rage are in this sense, a reaction to severe and unbearable identity anxieties and a deep rooted identity crisis that only finds one solution: to be acted out violently.

But of course, it has to be stated that not every fundamentalist turns out to be a terrorist or has any inclinations towards terror. Pratt as well as all scholars in this field agree 'that religious fundamentalism may ... in certain circumstances produce a terrorist', but that this is not an inescapable destiny, because it needs a specific set of circumstances to turn a fundamentalist into a terrorist (Pratt, 2017, p. 442). What then are these circumstances that turn a fundamentalist into a terrorist? First let's have a more profound look at fundamentalism.

According to Summers (2006), Jones (2006) and Pratt (2017) fundamentalism can be understood as a movement that rejects the increasing secularization of the world and the disempowerment of religion in daily life. In this context, the persistent consequences of the Enlightenment are not only criticized, but in their totality disavowed, because growing individualization, rationality and individual liberties are not seen and experienced as a unique chance to create one's own life and satisfy one's own needs, but these liberties are seen and experienced as an unbearable threat, ending up – inevitably – in different ways of alienation from God's will and expectations. In this alienated world, in which life seems to be filled with too many liberties, desires and uncertainties and not enough containment, fundamentalism represents a promising hope, because it pledges:

(1) to offer certainty, guidance and orientation,
(2) to offer a space of belonging and containment in the midst of growing complexities and globalization,
(3) to fulfill the need for an authority (a credo, a book or god) leaving no doubts, representing absolute, non-negotiable truths,
(4) to fulfill the need for identification and options to merge and bond symbiotically,
(5) to fulfill the desire for perfection, offering integrity and completeness without any need for changes or corrections,
(6) to fulfill the need for simplicity, offering explanations that reduce the complexity of reality, including bold and simple principles that are applicable everywhere, to everybody and at all times (Hole, 2004).

These all-embracing necessities that fundamentalism promises to fulfill according to Hole (2004) deliver an impressive idea of what is so attractive about fundamentalism. It seems like a manual that offers everything a helpless human being might need in times of crisis. However, the complexity of this list offers, at the same time, significant evidence of the gravity of a crisis that shines through from underneath, showing plainly that indeed these deep rooted hopes and desires cannot be fulfilled in any modern society. Is fundamentalism then the 'therapy' for the wrong diagnosis of the world's misery, offering the fulfillment of desires instead of reflection and enhancement of the capacity to critically analyze the situation? Let's have a look at the explanations of Kepel.

Gilles Kepel – God's revenge

Kepel's analysis of fundamentalism allows us a profound understanding of fundamentalist ways of thinking and of deeply rooted mentality structures.

He states that fundamentalist followers are by no means only the destitute, the poor, and the illiterate, but many of them have a college education and belong to the technical elite of their respective countries. According to Kepel (1993), fundamentalists in Muslim, Jewish and Christian societies criticize mainly the internal disintegration of society and the lack of a comprehensive perspective for the future. They do not believe in any secular morality, because they are convinced that this morality does not exist. Instead they believe that a world based on rationality and without God has not produced any values at all. They are convinced that the subsequent crisis shows nothing but the insubstantiality of secular utopia, this being expressed in two ways: In the West as egoism of spectacular consumption and in countries outside of Europe, the US and Japan, as repressive administration of poverty in combination with willful negligence of investments into human society. Religious fundamentalism refuses any compliance with secular constraints of society in order to bear witness for a different world in which mutually experienced solidarity is based on shared religious principles.

As Kepel (1993) further explains, the fundamentalist diagnosis of the world's crisis can be summarized as follows: The crisis in and of the world, of modern society and of modern man is a result of the loss of faith in God. Since modern man has moved away from God and abandoned him, the subsequent reaction necessarily produced severe experiences of social crisis (political instability, social conflicts, ethnic wars) natural disasters (droughts, tsunamis, earth quakes) and destitution (poverty, unemployment, corruption). Therefore, the only way to resolve this all-encompassing crisis, the disasters and destitution is to return to God and to his laws. This return has to be radical and has to be realized without any compromise and with complete intransigency, absolute obedience and submission. Doubts have to be banned from thought and emotion, faith is a matter of the heart and not a matter of rationality or reflection. One of the perpetrators of the 1993 bombing of the World Trade Center is reported to have told a journalist some time before: 'The soul of religion that is what is missing' (Juergensmeier, 2000, p. 69). This return to God implies as a consequence a radical rupture with all secular structures of modern ways of life and a complete subordination of rationality under the faith of God. This urging and non-questionable desire to return to God does not include, rather excludes any transformative action. The process of returning to God is therefore always an act of breaking with one's old life habits (as George Bush, jun. once put it: 'Good bye to Jack Daniels, hello to Jesus'), but sometimes also connected with belligerent action, bloodshed and the phantasy of purification. Kepel (1993) concludes that religious fundamentalism serves in this sense as a highly efficient method of a long lasting, but distorted social therapy. A therapy that calms down and quietens those that feel unrestful, ambivalent, insecure, but is repressive instead of empowering or emancipatory. In order to get close to God again, all resources are justified, be it modern media and technology, warfare or bombs.

There cannot be any doubt: The driving motivation behind the desire to return to God is more than just a simple decision to return to God, it is wrapped up in a phantasy of a reunion with God (Jones, 2006). In fact, and as Jones (2006) explains, it is the desire to achieve an explosive merger with a transcendent, awesome Father, God: 'The desire for an experience of union with a transcendental or divine reality appears as fundamental in virtually every religion' (Jones, 2006, p. 178). We might add: in patriarchal monotheism in general. But 'what is unique to fanatical religions is the linkage of the desire for spiritual reunion with violence, especially the violence of sacrificial killing or apocalyptic purification. It may be this linkage of a well-nigh universal and powerful spiritual desire with the themes of bloody sacrifice and purification through violence that turns spiritual longing into terrorist action' (Jones, 2006, p. 179). This describes the conjunction between terror and fundamentalism, meaning that underlying terror is always a fundamentalist (religious or political) attitude and conviction. This also means that terror without fundamentalism is hardly possible.

Jones further explains that this desire to merge with God implies the phantasy of becoming God oneself. The 'desire for God overwhelms all connections between human beings. The result is a detachment from empathic connections between human beings and their replacement by a totalizing connection with God alone. By identifying with God and what is supposed to be God's perspective, other human beings appear small and insignificant' (Jones, 2006, p. 182). All fundamentalist religions therefore focus on obedience, submission and purification, because they consider this the only possibility to earn divine favors. And as Jones critically adds, these are basically 'the central themes of a patriarchal religion' (Jones, 2006, p. 182). As Freud already pointed out in Totem and Taboo, the root of every religion is a 'longing for the father' (Freud, 1913, p. 148) and 'at bottom God is nothing other than an exalted father' (Freud, 1913, p. 47).

Wanting to be like God or even becoming God oneself is of course a powerful and omnipotent phantasy that covers all individual or social misery. This phantasy seems to be quite often connected with the experience of a severe personal or social crisis, and with disasters and destitution. This experience of a seemingly never-ending crisis produces feelings of shame and humiliation. Jones (2006) mentions in this context that for years psychology has emphasized the connections between shame, humiliation and violence. These conjunctions seem to be especially relevant for males (Gilligan, 1996; Miller, 1993), especially young, adolescent, and post-adolescent males.

Looking at the overall mortality rate for young men, it becomes evident that the mortality rate for young men increases almost sixfold between 10 to 14 years of age and 20–24 years of age. 'Although males 10–14 years of age have only a slightly greater mortality rate than females ... those 20–24 years of age have almost three times the mortality rate of females (142/100,000 vs. 48.2/100,000). Most of these deaths are due to unintentional injuries (motor vehicle crashes), suicide and homicide, all of which are often associated with alcohol and substance abuse' (Westwood & Pinzon, 2008). These dates and facts confirm the psychoanalytic thesis that male adolescent development is considered to be a phase of high risk. Could it therefore be that sacrificing oneself, and in some cases even one's victim, is a way to 'resolve' a severe adolescent crisis by sanctifying or purifying both? Or put in a different way: Sacrificing and killing oneself (and the victim) seems in some cases the only way out of an unbearable and unsolvable adolescent crisis. In this sense, terror could be considered a radical and violent male adolescent strategy to overcome a deep-rooted adolescent crisis, connected with shame and humiliation by killing oneself and/or others. This strategy would be driven by the desire to prove that at least this act of violence is not only an act of purification, but also one decisive last act of (self-) destructive empowerment.

These considerations are reinforced by the findings of Martin Riesebrodt (1990) in his book 'Fundamentalism as patriarchal protest movement' (translated from the German edition). He describes how modern societies with their social liberties, gender equality laws and secular ways of life are continuously threatening and disavowing patriarchal values, traditions and socially based patriarchal structures. This is not only true for Muslim societies, but a phenomenon on a global scale. Patriarchy in most societies worldwide has lost in different degrees, influence, power and control on almost all levels of society and especially within the family. Young men with higher education and with a professional and technological background have mostly replaced traditional male dominated craft and trade milieus (but in many cases find themselves unemployed albeit their higher education) and women have left their place in the family to study and work by entering in hitherto male dominated business and politics. The individual male experience of having lost the historically exclusive right to a self-determined existence is the basis of shame and humiliation and this individual experience is magnified by a general global crisis. According to Riesebrodt (1990) the turn to fundamentalism helps to at least slow down tendencies of dissolving patriarchal structures, because fundamentalist religious communities offer an alternative to the continuously increasing processes of acceleration by promoting spirituality, community and solidarity, and rejecting rapid social change that comes along with globalization, increased ethnic plurality, and individualism.

But in addition to this capacity to slow down tendencies of dissolving patriarchal structures Islamic fundamentalism has something very special to offer to young male adolescents with a Muslim background.

Male adolescence and identity crisis

Leuzinger-Bohleber and Lebiger-Vogel (2016) include in their book about migration, early parenthood and the transmission of trauma, an article about the radicalization of young male adolescents. They point out that all of the young jihadist fighters who had left Europe for Syria were known to have passed through stages of severe identity crises before they left their homes. Referring to early research about adolescence by Freud (1905, 1952) and Erikson (1979), who all agreed that adolescence was inherently a time of disturbance and psychological confusion, Leuzinger-Bohleber and Lebiger-Vogel (2016) point to the fact that severe forms of adolescent identity crises in almost all cases correspond with early childhood neglect and significant attachment difficulties. Csef (2017) emphasizes in his study of young jihadist fighters that 70% of all adolescents who went to Syria to fight with the troops of the Islamic State could be described by four criteria: Male, Muslim, migratory background and severe experiences of failure and frustration in their background, failure referring specifically to unemployment, criminal activities, disappointing peer relationships, precarious social and economic conditions in their families and a severe identity crisis. Many of these young men had experienced the separation of their parents, suicidal attempts of mothers and educational failures - insecure or missing attachment experiences leaving them alone with their anxieties, desires, needs and life's challenges (Csef, 2017). A significant number of young girls – in fact two thirds – who went to Syria in order to get married to an IS fighter, had experienced sexual abuse and violations that had never been reported to the police or processed by courts of justice (Bouzar, 2016). Also, in the case of young women, the refuge to IS is motivated by strong adolescent identity crises and the experience of injustice and social betrayal.

Approximately 80 000 young men worldwide (and some women as well) have ventured to Syria to support troops of the Islamic State. The promise and expectation to rebuild the Kalifate and participate in the recreation of the 'Golden Age of Islam' are highly seductive and promising for those who come from Muslim and war-torn, poverty stricken and politically repressive societies in the Near and Middle East, and for those who come as Muslims or migrants from Western societies with the experience of social exclusion, shame and humiliation.

The experience of being excluded and therefore feeling humiliated and shamed reinforces the desire to venture out of one's own society in search of a better, more promising social group with stricter rules and regulations, offering adventure and excitement, but at the same time containment for inner and outer turmoil, disappointment and frustration. This strong desire and need for attachment, orientation and containment is a strong motivation to seek a fundamentalist community or environment. A political and/or religious community like IS promises the possibility to re-enact narcissistic merger phantasies with an almighty object, and represents a space of purity, holiness and homogeneity. Additionally, the religious community re-activates sibling rivalry, reinforcing the rage against everybody who does not belong, emphasizing splitting tendencies and the feeling of one's own superiority (Bohleber, 1992). These phantasies help the male adolescent to survive an identity crisis, because the narcissistic depletion of his self is avoided by the refuge into phantasies of grandiosity and through the hallucinatory fusion with God, the Almighty. This hallucinatory fusion is usually connected with suicidal phantasies, with self-sacrifice and with violence (Leuzinger-Bohleber & Lebiger-Vogel, 2016). But what makes this phantasy of grandiosity even more attractive for the young adolescent Muslim terrorist is the expectation of sexual fulfillment: In heaven 72 virgins are waiting for him. This expectation liberates him from any pressure to find a wife, liberates him from his sexual desires, from the fear and threat of being rejected and subsequently feeling shamed and humiliated by a woman.

This sexual component is vital when it comes to the conjunction of terror and religious fundamentalism and male Muslim adolescence. The hallucinatory fusion with God, the phantasies of sexual grandiosity and potency, the avoidance of shame and humiliation all serve to ignore and finally avoid the challenges of any regular adolescent development. The usually conflictive modification of internalized parental images during the adolescent process is substituted by the hallucinatory fusion with God; the ambivalence of sexual desire and the desire to be loved by a woman and the fear of possible rejection is substituted by the phantasy of 72 virgins already waiting for him, without having to choose or proving his virility; the necessity to learn, to study, to take decisions and prepare for the hardships of real life, also connected with potential failures, maybe even with shame and humiliation are avoided by a violent suicidal act that kills himself and usually others, eliminating doubts, uncertainties, complexities, ambivalences, possible failures and promising sanctification and purification.

Young men, who enter the risky adolescent developmental phase and have not experienced secure attachment during early childhood, are neither able nor capable of separating from their internalized parental images and modifying the relationship with their parents in order to build up an autonomous sense of one self and secure identity. A young adolescent, who has never experienced secure attachment as a child, cannot separate later on in life as a young adult from internalized parental images. There are, at best, only fragments and unintegrated, fragile images. The only solution that seems left in this case, is a violent and bloody merger with God, the ultimate rationale aiming to fill the void left by the missing or failed attachment in early childhood. Adolescence then turns out to be a trap, the challenge cannot be met, and the step into adulthood fails. The suicidal terrorist act offers liberation and fulfillment: at least in this suicidal act of terror, the terrorist – at last – is not alone, killing himself and others at the same time. Only by dying does he finally connect to others, who are forced to share his death.

The essence of this experience appears clearly in a description of Jones (2006), who tells us about a Palestinian recruiter, who talks about his method of recruitment of suicide bombers: 'We focus his attention on Paradise, on being in the presence of Allah, on meeting the Prophet Muhammad, on interceding for his loved ones so that they too can be saved from the agonies of Hell' (Hassan, 2001, p. 40). The agonies of hell are for many young men adolescence and the reality of growing up in a liberal, non-patriarchal society that demands individual performance, individual responsibilities and the ability to bear ambivalence, uncertainty, complex realities and risky challenges.

Summary

Terror, fundamentalism and failed male adolescent developments seem to be a significant conjunction that helps to understand terror from a psychoanalytic and psychological point of view. This suggests that male adolescence implies a high risk factor for possible terroristic acts of violence. I propose that missing attachment experiences in early childhood, precarious economic situations in the family, frustrations in peer friendships and the experience of severe failures in school, all lead to a psychopathological identity crisis in adolescence. Fundamentalist communities offer help and support to all those who look for attachment and containment, promising a fusion with God. Thus religious fundamentalism offers a way out of the challenges of a liberal society and moreover, a traditional male identity that does not know ambivalence, anxieties, fears or rivalry with women.

In conclusion, what is needed are in depth investigations of male adolescent developments, especially to explore the different aspects that eventually lead to psychopathological identity crises in young men. This paper offers preliminary thoughts about these issues that need a more profound empirical research basis. But for more effective political action and educational prevention programs it is clear that young male adolescents are a group that need more attention and more support in order to avoid them venturing into fundamentalist ideologies and communities and from there possibly into terrorist action.

Disclosure statement

No potential conflict of interest was reported by the author.

References

Armstrong, K. (2000). *The battle for God: Fundamentalism in Judaism, Christianity and Islam*. London: HarperCollins.

Beier, M. (2006). On the psychology of violent Christian fundamentalism: Fighting to matter ultimately. *Psychoanalytic Review, 93*, 301–328.

Blos, P. (1979). *The adolescent passage*. Madison, WI: International University Press.

Bohleber, W. (1992). Nationalismus, Fremdenhaß und Antisemitismus. Psychoanalytische Überlegungen [Nationalism, Xenophobia and Antisemitism. Psychoanalytic Considerations]. *Psyche Zeitschrift für Psychoanalyse, 46*, 689–709.

Bouzar, D. (2016). Wege aus der Rekrutierungsfalle. *Gehirn & Geist, 29*, 3.

Csef, H. (2017). Faszination Dschihad. Was junge Deutsche beim IS suchen und finden. *Journal für Psychologie, 25*, 205–224.

Erikson, E. H. (1979). *Identität und Lebenszyklus* [Identiy and life cycle]. Frankfurt: Suhrkamp.

Freud, A. (1952). Adolescence. *Psychoanalytic Study of the Child, 13*, 255–278.

Freud, S. (1913). Totem and taboo. *The standard edition of the complete psychological works of Sigmund Freud* (Vol. XIII). London: Hogarth Press.

Freud, S. (1905) Three essays on the theory of sexuality. *The standard edition of the complete psychological works of Sigmund Freud* (Vol. VII). London: Hogarth Press.

Gilligan, J. (1996). *Violence*. New York, NY: Random House.

Hassan, N. (2001). An arsenal of believers. *The New Yorker*, pp. 36–41.

Hole, G. (2004). *Fanatismus. Der Drang zum Extrem und seine psychischen Wurzeln*. Gießen: Psychosozial-Verlag.

Jones, J. W. (2006). Why does religion turn violent? A psychoanalytic exploration of religious terrorism. *Psychoanalytic Review, 93*, 168–190.

Juergensmeier, M. (2000). *Terror in the mind of God*. Berkeley, CA: University of California Press.

Kepel, G. (1993). *The revenge of God. The resurgence of Islam, Christianity, and Judaism in the modern world*. University Park, PA: Penn State University Press.

Laufer, M. (1965). Assessment of adolescent disturbances. The application of Anna Freud's diagnostic profile. *Psychoanalytic Study of the Child, 20*, 99–123.

Leuzinger-Bohleber, M., & Lebiger-Vogel, J. (Eds.). (2016). *Migration, frühe Elternschaft und die Weitergabe von Traumatisierungen* [Migration, early parenthood and the transmission of Traumatisations]. Stuttgart: Klett-Cotta.

Miller, W. (1993). *Humiliation and other essays on honor, social discomfort, and violence*. Ithaca, NY: Cornell University Press.

Pratt, D. (2017). Religion and terrorism: Christian fundamentalism and extremism. *Terrorism and Political Violence, 22*, 438–456. doi:10.1080/09546551003689399

Riesebrodt, M. (1990). *Fundamentalismus als patriarchale Protestbewegung. Amerikanische Protestanten (1910–28 und iranische Schiiten (1961–79) im Vergleich.* [Fundamentalism as Patriarchal Protest Movement]. Tübingen: J.C.B. Mohr.

Riesebrodt, M. (1993). *Pious passion: The emergence of modern fundamentalism in the United States and Iran.* Berkeley, CA: University of California Press.

Stein, R. (2009). *For love of the father. A psychoanalytic study of religious terrorism.* Stanford, CA: Stanford University Press.

Summers, F. (2006). Fundamentalism, psychoanalysis, and psychoanalytic theories. *Psychoanalytic Review, 93*, 329–352.

Westwood, M., & Pinzon, J. (2008). Adolescent male health. Retrieved April 13, 2017, from https://www.ncbi.nlm.nih.gov/pmc/articles/PMC2528816/

Dreaming of Columbine: exploring an offender's preoccupation with the Columbine Massacre

Maktuno Suit

In 1999, two students, Eric Harris and Dylan Kleobold, armed with guns and explosives killed 12 peers, one teacher and wounded more than 20 others before taking their own lives. Since that date, society has sought to understand what drove these young men to commit such an act of hate and violence as well as the copycat school shootings, cult fascination and fandom associated with the perpetrators. In this paper, I discuss an offender on licence in the community who developed an obsession with the perpetrators and narrative of the Columbine Massacre alongside expressing an interest in participating in violent Islamist extremism – the use of violent tactics for achieving perceived Islamic goals. Furthermore, I explore my counter-transference as a psychotherapist conducting a risk-focused therapeutic intervention with this personality-disordered man. This paper will highlight the importance of using a psychoanalytic perspective to explore the link between an individual's psychopathology and their fascination with the Columbine Massacre. It will also provide useful reflections for understanding the unconscious appeal of violent extremist narratives and ideologies.

Introduction

In this paper, I describe my experience of working with 27-year-old Luke – not his real name – who had been referred to a community forensic personality disorder service by his probation officer. I was employed as a Clinical Practitioner with psychotherapeutic expertise in a multi-disciplinary team. Our primary function was to work with high-risk offenders who had been screened into the National Offender Management Service's Offender Personality Disorder Pathway. As a service we conducted comprehensive risk assessments and interventions for personality-disordered offenders over a time-limited period of 12 months.

Luke's index offence had been that of approaching and subsequently stalking a female that he was interested in dating. After feeling rejected by her he began sending murderous threats via social media through an online profile, where he assumed the alter-ego identity of Columbine killer Eric Harris. He had received a custodial sentence for this, and after a brief time had been transferred to a medium secure unit (MSU) for psychiatric assessment. Once admitted he was assessed for psychosis and Autistic Spectrum Disorder (ASD) – but he failed to meet the threshold for a psychotic illness or an ASD diagnosis. Luke was eventually discharged from the MSU with a diagnosis of antisocial personality disorder with narcissistic and schizoid traits.

After being discharged from the MSU, Luke began to regularly communicate with mental health professionals and his probation officer about his interest in the Columbine Massacre and expressed sympathies with Eric Harris and Dylan Kleobold's murderous acts and motivations. His fascination with Columbine caused heightened anxieties about his risk, which were exacerbated due to fears that he had been radicalized during his time in custody – where he had converted to Islam and openly expressed interest in becoming a jihadist fighter. Due to the climate of fear of radicalization and extremism in wider society, the systemic countertransference to Luke had been one of fear and moral indignation for his interests and beliefs. Consequently, this led to increased surveillance, multiple agencies becoming involved and strict license conditions being imposed, which caused Luke to become increasingly non-compliant and disengaged with his probation officer. Luke was referred to our service to help his probation officer and other criminal justice agencies better understand his risk of reoffending. Furthermore, they were anxious to ascertain the likelihood of him acting on his 'extreme' interests and requested consultative advice for how to effectively manage him in the community.

After an initial assessment period of three months, it was decided that Luke would be offered a nine-month structured piece of work that focused on relationships and helping him to engage with positive social activities in his local area to reduce his levels of social isolation. As his named professional, I brought to our work a psychoanalytic understanding of Luke's offending and a curiosity about the unconscious functions of his interest in extreme violent narratives. We initially worked together in a structured way for the first few months and then decided to adopt a more unstructured, psychotherapeutic way of working to contain and explore his offence paralleling behaviour that continually threatened our working relationship.

In this paper, I will explore Luke's 'extreme' sympathies and offending behaviour from a psychoanalytic perspective, attempting to understand the unconscious meaning behind them, and look to understand how 'that which is unbearable to think finds its expression in action' (Yakeley, 2007). This will help us to understand the complexities of his psychopathology and, more generally, illuminate why an individual might align him/herself with an 'extremist' narrative. In writing this, I have found Gilligan's (1996) work on the role of humiliation in violence useful in helping me understand Luke's aggressive response to being rejected and his identification with the Columbine killers and their murderous rage. Kohut (1971) and his work exploring the link between the narcissistic personality and alter-egos, and Glasser's (1979) concept of the 'core complex' have also been useful in terms of his offending and destructive pattern of relating to others.

The Columbine Stalker

Luke's forensic history extends over a period of 12 months in his early 20s. His first offence was a criminal charge for harassment and stalking after he had become pathologically attached to a young woman who worked at a betting shop he had been frequenting. Luke, an avid gambler, had been visiting the shop and after becoming interested in her he began spending hours staring at her behind the counter. When she eventually challenged him about his behaviour he left the shop; but when she left work that night he was outside of the shop and followed her home.

Over the next two weeks, Luke waited outside the book-makers until the woman eventually called the police who intervened and gave him words of advice. Three days later, he was found again outside the betting shop and was served with a Harassment Warning Notice. Despite this, two weeks later, he was found outside the shop again. He had also been contacting the victim and her sister, sending several messages, including a threat to kill them through a Facebook account with a profile picture of Eric Harris. He was arrested and released on bail, after which he sent a threatening message to the woman's boyfriend, who had confronted him on a previous occasion in the betting shop. He was then remanded into custody and later received a short suspended custodial sentence.

A Restraining Order was imposed and after breaking this he was placed in custody for 12 months. After his release he was later convicted of harassment of a female housing worker, where he displayed similar stalking behaviour – incessantly contacting her outside office hours and placing an arm around her during an appointment. He was put back in custody and during this time he converted to Islam and began expressing violent Islamist extremist views. These included inciting others to commit suicide bombings and an expression of interest in travelling to Afghanistan to fight alongside the Taliban. Following observation he was transferred to an MSU for assessment, from where he was later discharged into the community.

When our service first received Luke as a referral, reports indicated that clinicians had been undecided about his diagnosis and disorientated by his presentation and highly challenging interpersonal difficulties. These reports accurately mirrored my first experience meeting Luke in a London probation office with his probation officer on a cold, wet winter afternoon. He had been discharged from the MSU a month previously and a female clinical psychologist and I had arrived to conduct a clinical interview as part of our initial risk assessment process. This first meeting provided me with some useful insights into Luke's psychopathology. Wearing flip flops and sporting a long wispy beard, he struggled to make eye contact with us and shifted anxiously in his chair as his offender manager made introductions across the table. After he left the room, Luke became aggressively non-compliant and withholding and I became aware of how he was experiencing our interview as intrusive as he openly expressed his distrust about how the information we were attempting to gain might be used against him. He also demanded to know more about us before he would continue the session and became fixated with finding out the zodiac sign of my female colleague. She experienced this as intruding upon a professional boundary and she refused to disclose it. Luke then continued to push further, until we eventually decided to end the session early due to the level of discomfort she was experiencing. Early on, it was evident that Luke was fiercely resistant to feeling intruded upon alongside having a tendency to antagonize others through intruding upon their personal boundaries.

Personal background

Luke was born in the Caribbean into a wealthy family with an Asian mother and English father. He was an only child and grew up with infrequent contact with three half siblings from his father's previous marriage. He reported having a positive and enjoyable relationship with his father, who died in his early 20s, and an ambivalent and strained relationship with his mother whose parenting he described as shifting between being intrusive and detached.

Luke's family came to the UK when he was six because of his father's work. He had difficulty making friends at primary school and attended several secondary schools. He was then sent to boarding school where he was bullied – a traumatic experience that he adamantly refused to talk about. After passing his GCSEs in boarding school he returned to college in London but failed to complete his A-levels.

In his early twenties, Luke's father died, which he struggled to process emotionally. He talked about losing someone close to him with whom he used to play board games and discuss topical issues in the news. During his teenage years his father was retired which meant that he spent considerable amounts of time with him. Shortly after his father's death Luke left the family home due to his increasingly volatile relationship with his mother. Luke always struggled to build relationships with others and had never experienced an intimate relationship with a woman. He was socially isolated and used the internet to relate to others through anonymous chat rooms and websites where he assumed alter-ego identities. He also had an interest in gambling and playing chess.

Luke's first contact with psychiatric services came shortly after his father's death when he was admitted to hospital after being arrested at a synagogue. He had been attempting to enter the building, and threatened to blow it up after being refused entry. During his first admission he openly disclosed to clinicians that he had a fascination with the Columbine Massacre and strongly identified with the perpetrators – Eric Harris and Dylan Kleobold. Over the two-year period when he first became involved with the criminal justice system he committed offences of stalking and harassment, and consequently spent two periods in prison and time in a secure hospital. When he was discharged to the community he began living in private rented accommodation, and it was at this point that our service began working with him on licence, alongside probation staff.

After completing the initial assessment and starting his intervention focused on relationships, he started to spend more time in his mother's home due to bullying and threats of harm made towards him by a fellow resident in his accommodation. However, due to the strain of his relationship with his mother he was hospitalized under Section 2 of the Mental Health Act for psychiatric assessment after she began to feel threatened by him and called the police. Whilst work was undertaken with Luke over a 12-month period, he was arrested and hospitalized on several occasions, for incidents that included: an altercation with a passenger on a train who tried to prevent him from following a group of young women he was attempting to befriend, and an argument with a fellow train passenger attempting to prevent him from making racist slurs towards other passengers and shouting anti-British/anti-government comments. Luke was a man who had a history of aligning himself with antisocial ideas and sentiments that existed outside of mainstream conventions and levels of acceptance. The foremost of these was his obsession with the Columbine Killings that this paper will go on to explore.

The Columbine narrative

Prior to the Columbine Massacre, Eric Harris and Dylan Kleobold created diaries and videos that would be read and watched in the aftermath of their mass killing. In this respect, they were creative writers that helped create the 'Columbine Myth' that has become embedded in popular culture as the story of two young men who achieved murderous revenge against school athletes who bullied and tormented them (Thomas, Levine, Cloherty, & Date, 2014; Rico, 2015). Freud writes in 'Creative Writers and Daydreaming' (1907) that the stories of creative writers can evoke unconscious feelings in us – much like he himself found resonance with the Greek Myth 'Oedipus Rex' (1900) and identified his own repressed unconscious desires embedded within the story. Luke identified himself consistently with violent, extreme narratives and the script and characters of the 'Columbine Myth' held particular meaning for him.

Luke described first becoming interested in the Columbine Massacre at a time when he was being bullied in secondary school and he watched Michael Moore's 2002 film 'Bowling for Columbine'. Since then, he had talked to his probation officer about his interest in the killings. He described how the actions of the Columbine Killers resonated with him due to his own experiences of bullying, and stated that he could sympathize with their feelings of rejection and anger. Luke's angry emotions at being rejected were prevalent in his index offence where he experienced the narcissistic injury of a woman's rejection. Consequently, his rage was activated to protect his weak ego and fragile self-esteem, and he responded through sending his victim a murderous Facebook message where he assumed the alter-ego of Eric Harris. During our initial assessment, he expanded on these murderous fantasies telling me how at times he dreamed about driving a car and running over as many people as possible. The work of Gilligan (1996) is useful for understanding Luke's violent response in his index offence as a need to ward off narcissistic injuries and overwhelming feelings of shame and humiliation.

Luke described 'fantasizing' about the Columbine Massacre when he felt low in mood or suicidal, and described this experience as offering some cathartic relief for him. Luke had detailed insight into the killer's motivations, and emotional states at the time of committing the massacre. He revelled in this massacre as it perhaps represented his own unconscious desires, and he found relief and expression of them when he replayed Eric and Dylan's actions in his head. By engaging with the Columbine narrative Luke appeared to experience a clandestine excitement where he felt omnipotent in his act of anticipated violence. In fantasy, he was placed in a position of relative power and dominance towards others; where he could identify with the bullied Eric Harris and exact rageful revenge on his own high school and present day 'oppressors'.

Luke often struggled to put his feelings into words and used symbolism and analogies to communicate his emotional states. This perhaps helps us to understand how Luke might have used his disclosure of interest in the Columbine Massacre as a communicative vehicle; and rather than expressing his emotions, he presented professionals with a symbolic narrative to interpret. Kenneth Wright writes about this in his book 'Mirroring and Attunement: Self Realization in Psychoanalysis and Art' (2009) that explores the role of symbolism in expression of emotional states. When Luke was trying to share and communicate with others about his internal objects, that which is intangible and personal, he used different symbolic vehicles. With his stories and analogies he appeared to be 'dispatching a parcel containing a model of experience rather than sending a letter that simply describes it' (Wright, 2009, p. 106).

Perhaps Luke's primary difficulty was a language deficiency – that he lacked the words to tell people his emotional states and instead symbolized them. (Wright, 2009) His use of the Columbine narrative could be thought of as a cultural transitional object – a piece of art/poetry that 'retrieves and holds onto precious elements of experience' (Wright, 2009, p. 112). When words failed him, he often used detailed analogies or objects in the room to depict his emotional states, or comment on the dynamic that was prevalent in our working relationship. A good example of this was when I visited Luke on an acute psychiatric ward after he had been admitted following his altercation with a member of public on a train. He was initially non-compliant and dismissive when I asked questions or attempted to interact with him. In our work, it felt we had reached a point of impasse where his withholding of information and inherent distrust of me was making our working relationship untenable. After expressing my sense of frustration with his non-compliance, Luke jumped up out of his chair, picked up a whiteboard marker and drew a boat on a whiteboard. He said: 'I feel like we're on a boat and we are trying to get somewhere, but there are holes in it'. I responded by saying that perhaps he was referring to the notion that our relationship had holes in it, and it was important for us to explore what these difficulties were if we wanted to move forward. This led on to him being able to communicate how he had struggled to trust me and the close working relationship that I had with his probation officer. As is demonstrated here, Luke often used symbolic language to communicate his emotional states, and these acted as a bridge to understanding his internal world. Like his obsession with Columbine he used allegories or stories to explain and frame his emotional states.

The Columbine characters

Luke's connection with the Columbine narrative appeared to extend beyond sympathy and vicarious identification with Eric and Dylan's rejection and rage. Luke had alluded to having a 'special relationship' with the Columbine killers. During his first admission to hospital after threatening to blow up a synagogue, he told doctors that he wanted to get a gun and kill strangers to get into the minds of the Columbine killers. He said that he wanted to 'make bombs and kill strangers', and reported auditory hallucinations commanding him to kill other people. On another occasion, whilst in prison he talked about how Eric Harris had told him to defend himself from inmates who had threatened to hurt him. This could be likened to the special attachment that Eric and Dylan themselves felt towards Timothy McVeigh who perpetrated the Oklahoma bombings (Langman, 2009).

Kohut's work around the narcissistic personality and alter-egos is useful in terms of understanding the 'special attachment' that Luke had with Eric Harris. Kohut (1971, 1984) and Kohut & Wolf (1986) theorized about how pathological narcissism, deficits in interpersonal functioning and an incohesive sense of self emerge, when an individual fails to have their crucial developmental needs met. He described these as being an infant's 'self-object' needs for 'mirroring', 'idealization' and 'twinship' – which can be summarized as a desire to merge with the object. Kohut pointed out that 'fantasies, referring to a relationship with an alter ego or twin (or conscious wishes for such a relationship) are frequently encountered in the analysis of narcissistic personalities' (Kohut, 1971) and this perhaps helps us to understand Luke's narcissistic link to Eric Harris in fantasy. Kohut's ideas mirror Freud's notion that the 'double' (or the alter-ego) 'sprung from the primary narcissism which holds sway in the mind of the child' (Freud, 1909). Luke's identification with Eric Harris could be theorized as being a compensation for early attachment failures, with this reflecting his need for an idealized and omnipotent internal image of Eric whom he can identify with to the point of feeling associated with, or experience as a part of his mind. This could be reflective of his need for parental experiences he may not have had during the practicing sub-phase outlined by Mahler, Pine and Bergman (1973) in her theory of development. Luke's special relationship with Eric Harris could be understood as him attempting to satisfy an archaic hunger for self-object needs (Kohut, 1971) by forming a narcissistic link to an omnipotent alter-ego in fantasy. Alongside his desired relationship in fantasy with Eric Harris, Luke appears to seek relationships with others that meet his unfulfilled self-object needs. Notably, during our sessions on relationships Luke described how his idea of a good relationship was one that was co-dependent, mutual, secretive and perfect; this description reflects his profound longing for union and a blissful state of oneness and fusion.

It could be hypothesized that Luke's 'special attachment' to the Columbine killers is indicative of him suffering from psychosis in a psychoanalytic, rather than a psychiatric sense; where he becomes so psychologically fragmented that he loses the 'as if' quality to his identification with the Columbine killers and his alter-egos appear real to him. Perhaps, Luke's hallucinatory experiences and delusional ideas were reflective of defensive processes in play to guard against unbearable underlying feelings of victimization and extreme vulnerability. In line with the psychoanalytic approach to psychosis, to understand Luke's psychotic symptoms, 'attention should be paid to clarifying experiences of reality that the person has found unmanageable and, which have, through the psychosis, been dispensed with or altered, rather than contained, "digested" and integrated as in non-psychotic states' (Martindale & Summers, 2013).

Finally, Luke's vocal expression of interest in the Columbine Massacre also appeared to have an interpersonal function in terms of the emotions this evoked in professionals. He was particularly vocal with his probation officer, who was often horrified by his fascination and sympathies with the massacre. Perhaps, a function of Luke vocalizing his fascination with Columbine was the potent and intrusive effect it had on others. While I observed Luke talk about his views to his probation officer, he often appeared to revel in the moral reprehension and horrified reactions to his extreme views; which extended beyond Columbine to being supportive of violent terrorist incidents as well as President Donald Trump's extreme thoughts/actions in the run up to the 2016 US election. Moreover, Luke's disclosures about Columbine had the effect of bringing a socially isolated man into contact with multiple agencies consisting of concerned adults eager to understand his internal world. His probation officer often reported in consultative conversations that he would be kept awake at night preoccupied by a fear that Luke would potentially act on his violent obsessions. This is a good example of how his disclosures led to him being 'held in mind' by others – something that perhaps compensated for the lack of relational attunement he had experienced throughout his life.

Columbine in the consulting room

My interactions with Luke during our structured sessions exploring relationships provided me with further insights into his psychopathology and attachment difficulties. Over his first few months of engagement, I became aware of two contrasting presentations. At times Luke presented with a desire for an idealistic, un-boundaried relationship. On other occasions he appeared detached and disinterested in our sessions with an intense fear of being intruded upon. Initially, Luke was very keen to attend and would be eager to arrange our next meeting.

He would arrive in reception and make himself a cup of coffee, engaging with the receptionist in small talk with relaxed enjoyment. On these occasions, Luke would normally enter the room with the day's newspaper and started talking animatedly about something in the news. As we moved on to exploring his relationships, he would ask questions about my own experiences and at times it felt like he desperately wanted to understand how people managed difficult emotions and social situations. For example, on one occasion he was curious to know if I had ever been rejected and how I had dealt emotionally with that.

At other times he showed extreme reluctance to attend sessions and would be out of contact for a fortnight and make himself unable to meet at any of the times offered to him. Arranging a mutual time and date would be extremely difficult and he would arrive at a session in a defensive mood, resistant to any type of therapeutic engagement. In these sessions, Luke would ask personal questions but in what felt like a more intrusive and aggressive way. This shift from desiring informal engagement to aggressive detachment could be witnessed in a single session where he would be cooperative and engaged and then vehemently resist arranging another session, smiling as he rejected different times and dates that were offered to him. Throughout our work, Luke fiercely resisted arranging a regular date and time and would only commit to a session over the phone, a few days before meeting.

Glasser's 'core complex' (1979) is a useful way of conceptualizing Luke's behaviour that fluctuated between a desire for merging and fear of being alone and then the subsequent fear of annihilation and being engulfed. This is similar to Rey (1994) and his notion of the claustro-agoraphobic dilemma, where he describes patients that are not secure being with objects, or away from them, which then manifests as a constant push-pull dynamic within the transference. This dynamic reflected the relationship that he described with his mother between being intrusive or isolating. In his early life, Luke described a mother who both intensified these annihilatory anxieties using him to meet her own narcissistic needs and neglected his needs thus amplifying abandonment anxieties and aggression. Glasser theorized that aggression is a central component of the 'core complex' and that the loss of separate existence creates an aggressive reaction on the part of the ego; and that in order to preserve the self the object needs to be destroyed. He contends that for fear of losing the object and the comfort and security s/he provides, this aggression is libidinized and converted into sadism: 'the mother is therefore preserved and no longer threatened by total destruction, as the intention to destroy is converted to a desire to hurt and control' (Yakeley, 2007). Luke often presented with an 'intrusion anxiety' that others would control him in the same way that he experienced his mother, and perhaps he had a need to control our sessions to protect himself from feeling violently intruded upon.

I have found Bowlby's work on attachment (1973, 1988) useful in understanding Luke's behaviour as being reflective of an insecure preoccupied adult attachment style that created a push-pull dynamic in the relationships that he had with professionals including myself. This was evidenced by his clinginess and desire for closeness alongside a simultaneous distrust and desire to distance himself from me during our interactions. Luke's internal working models were reproduced within the analytic frame of our sessions and provided useful information related to his insecure attachment style. Luke fluctuated between resisting attachment and clinging to it, which could be very disorientating when relating to him. A major part of our work was focused on helping him to understand his pattern of relating to others, and his intrusive attacks on people's interpersonal boundaries – it was important to help him to think rather than act.

Clinical example

This is a clinical example of a session with Luke held at the offices of our forensic service. The session was scheduled to last sixty minutes and I had been meeting with him for six months by this point. It demonstrates how Luke's psychopathology manifested in our working relationship.

Luke arrived at his session 45 minutes early and called me when I was in the process of travelling in to the office from another appointment. When I later arrived we started the session at the agreed time. Luke began the session by talking about how he had been upset by an interaction with his probation officer who had stated that he was still a threat to females and at risk of intruding on their interpersonal boundaries. This led in to a discussion where I asked him to think about his recent behaviour on a hospital ward where he had been touching a female nursing staff's hair and following female psychologists around the ward. At this point, I was able to reflect on how he often acted the same way with me – pushing the boundaries of the session, intruding upon my time and struggling with the formal boundaries of our professional–client relationship. I also observed how these same dynamics were evident in his index offence. This interpretation resonated with him and we went on to discuss how sticking to the boundaries of our session would be important in terms of helping him to learn how to relate to people with boundaries. Luke stated that when he turned up at the wrong time he often thought that I might get angry and refuse to work with him. He commented on how he intentionally antagonized people and gained enjoyment from witnessing the emotional reaction he evoked in them. This was consistent with my own observations of how Luke often smirked and appeared to enjoy witnessing the impact his intrusions had upon me – whether that be through his erratic and unpredictable attendance or through the intrusive personal questions that he asked.

Concluding thoughts

When Luke was first referred to our service, his on-going fascination with the extreme violent narrative of the Columbine Massacre, and previous expression of interest in violent Islamist extremism led to criminal justice agencies increasing surveillance and imposing strict licence conditions to manage his risk in the community. Working with Luke, we were able to look beneath the surface of his extreme interests and bring a more psychologically informed approach to his management – identifying his key vulnerabilities and key risk factors.

As a clinician working with him I was able use my own countertransference and psychoanalytic expertise to better understand and explore the unconscious function of his extreme interests in light of his early attachment failures and unbearable feelings of shame/humiliation connected to the bullying and victimization he had experienced throughout his life. This paper has important implications in terms of the criminal justice system's approach to individuals expressing extreme, violent views; it demonstrates how an ability to work with the unconscious can be useful in terms of understanding an individual's alignment with extremist ideologies/narratives.

In the wake of recent terrorist attacks by violent Islamist extremists in Manchester (22 May 2017) and London (3 June 2017), it is important to look beneath the surface at the unconscious reasons why people might become aligned to extreme, violent narratives or ideologies. This paper demonstrates again the valuable contribution of forensic psychotherapeutic thinking and approaches to understanding inconceivable and irrational violent fantasies and acts. Furthermore, for those individuals that authorities have identified as being at risk of radicalization or extremism, this paper demonstrates how a psychologically informed approach to understanding risk and a person's offending will lead to more effective management of them in the community. Without this approach, we run the danger of agencies (as in Luke's case) engulfing individuals with intense supervision and multi-agency involvement that lead to non compliance and more difficulties managing risk.

This paper has also highlighted how a future investigation into the systemic countertransference of criminal justice agencies to individuals with extremist views would be a fruitful area of enquiry; especially in terms of thinking about its impact on risk management strategies. Moreover, it would be interesting in the light of this paper to further explore the psychological reasons for perpetrators of terrorist violence choosing to align themselves with violent extremist narratives and ideologies.

Disclosure statement

No potential conflict of interest was reported by the author.

References

Bowlby, J. (1973). *Separation anxiety and anger*. London: Perseus Books Groups.

Bowlby, J. (1988). *A secure base: Parent child attachment and healthy human development*. London: Perseus Books Groups.

Freud, S. (1900). *Interpretation of dreams*. London: Wordsworth Editions.

Freud, S. (1907). *Creative writers and daydreaming*. London: Penguin Books.
Freud, S. (1909). *The Uncanny*. London: Penguin Books.
Glasser, M. (1979). Some aspects of the role of aggression in the perversions. In I. Rosen (Ed.), *Sexual deviation* (2nd ed., pp. 270–305). Oxford: OUP.
Gilligan, J. (1996). *Violence: Reflections on our deadliest epidemic*. New York, NY: First Vintage Books Edition.
Kohut, H. (1971). *The analysis of the self: A systematic approach to the psychoanalytic treatment of narcissistic personality disorders*. Chicago, IL: The University of Chicago Press.
Kohut, H., & Wolf, E. S. (1986). The disorders of the self and their treatment: An outline. In A. P. Morrison (Ed.), *Essential papers on Narcissism* (pp. 175–196). New York, NY: New York University of Press Books.
Kohut, H. (1984). *How does analysis cure?* Chicago, IL: The University of Chicago Press.
Langman, P. (2009). *Why kids kill: Inside the mind of school shooters*. New York, NY: Palgrave Macmillan.
Mahler, M. S., Pine, F., & Bergman, A. (1973). *The psychological birth of the human infant*. New York, NY: Basic Books.
Martindale, B., & Summers, A. (2013). The psychodynamics of psychosis. *Advances in Psychiatric Treatment, 19*, 124–131.
Rico, A. (2015). Fans of Columbine Shooters Eric Harris and Dylan Kleobold. *Transformative Works and Cultures*, no. 20. Retrieved from https://doi.org/10.3983/twc.2015.0671
Rey, H. (1994). *Universals of psychoanalysis in the treatment of psychotic and borderline states*. London: Free Association Books.
Thomas, P., Levine, M., Cloherty, J., & Date, J. (2014, October 7). Columbine shootings' grim legacy: More than 50 school attacks, plots. *ABC News*. Retrieved from https://abcnews.go.com/US/columbine-shootings-grim-legacy-50-school-attacks-plots/story?id=26007119
Wright, K. (2009). *Mirroring and attunement: Self realization in psychoanalysis and art*. London: Routledge.
Yakeley, J. (2007). Psychoanalytic contributions to risk assessment and management. In D. Morgan & S. Ruszczynsky (Eds.), *Lectures on violence, perversion and delinquency: The Portman Papers* (pp. 70–93). London: Karnac Books.

Pathways into terrorism: the Good, the Bad and the Ugly

Monica Lloyd and Pamela Kleinot

This paper contains the reflections of the first author as a forensic psychologist working with convicted terrorists in prison between 2008 and 2011, and subsequently as an academic and government consultant in this field. The task of making sense of this learning has been helped by a psychoanalytic understanding of the causes of terrorism by the second author who is a psychotherapist and group analyst. Psychoanalytic processes of defences, splitting and projection throw light on the potential unconscious thoughts, feelings and behaviour of those who resort to terrorism. Two broad groups are identified whose motivations are ostensibly noble cause and criminality respectively, but whose involvement also serves to avenge their personal humiliations and feelings of injustice that are projected into a political cause. A third group is also described of mainly lone actors motivated by pathological narcissism. It is proposed that terrorism manifests as a political phenomenon but is also a form of communication that reveals much about the state of mind of those who choose to become involved.

Background

Following the London suicide bombings of the transport system in 7/7, the UK Government passed legislation criminalising behaviours considered to be preparatory to terrorism or which glorified terrorism in an attempt to disrupt terrorist plotting within the UK.[1] This brought into custody a number of offenders who were in varying degrees engaged in jihadi ideology, not all of whom were intending to commit terrorist offences at the time of their arrest. It was important therefore to develop a transparent and defensible methodology for making discriminations between them so that they could be managed in a way that was proportionate to their risk of harm. With the country still galvanised by the terror induced by these attacks, levels of risk aversion in prisons were high. All terrorist prisoners were classified as high risk by default, and the bar for declassification was set very high.

Individual psychopathology

The literature about what engages individuals in terrorism and the evidence for psychopathology in terrorists is confused; there are many definitions of terrorism and suggestions for how terrorism or terrorists might be classified, but no single pathway or consensus about their psychology. Research by psychiatrists and psychoanalysts that tried to make sense of totalitarianism and the genocide of the Second World War focused on psychopathy, narcissistic personality disorder and authoritarianism as possible causes. In contrast, the political science literature concluded that terrorist violence was the product of rational decision-making to bring about political change within asymmetrical power structures when other means were unavailable. Crenshaw (1981) famously concluded that 'the outstanding common characteristic of terrorists is their normality' (p. 390) and Arendt (1963) came to a similar conclusion in referring to the *'banality of evil'* in the title of her book referring to Adolf Eichmann's presentation at his trial for his actions as the architect of the Holocaust.

Corner, Gill, and Mason (2016) collated multiple psychiatric epidemiological studies to calculate the prevalence of diagnosed mental disorders in the general population and compare them to the prevalence of the same disorders among lone-actor and group-actor terrorists. They identified higher recorded levels of schizophrenia, autistic spectrum disorder and unspecified personality disorder in lone actors than in the general population, but lower recorded levels of any disorder at all in group actors. The latter, however, is likely to be a result of the absence of psychiatric assessment of group actors rather than an indicator of their superior mental health.

The disorders that are over-represented among lone actors are those associated with pervasive problems of personal and social adjustment, such as odd and eccentric behaviour, communication deficits, idiosyncratic beliefs, difficulties in relationships and social isolation. In earlier research Corner and Gill (2015) identified a high preponderance of single-issue ideologies in lone actors alongside highly personal grievances linked to political aims. Though a causal role between these difficulties and extremist violence cannot be assumed, for those who have failed to find their place in society, an ideology that provides an explanation for their difficulties and locates the responsibility elsewhere may be seized upon and become something of a fixation over time.

However, although helpful in dispelling the truism that there is no psychopathology in terrorists this says little about the larger proportion of group actors. In truth, studies have not been done that systematically assess the presence of diagnosable mental disorders in group actor terrorists, or more specifically in those fulfilling the different roles of leaders, followers, enforcers, funders, bomb planters or suicide bombers that are likely to attract different personalities and motivations. Self-evidently, socio-economic inequality and political oppression are insufficient explanations in themselves as this would apply to a much larger number than the few who become terrorists. As Miller (2006) asserts 'Something then beyond mere adversity, turns a person into a terrorist' (p. 255).

Over time, the first author's casework in prisons identified vulnerabilities such as grievance and a sense of injustice, identity and status issues, thwarted ambitions, a breakdown in relationships (often with the father), poor social adjustment and a general lack of well-being. Dialogue revealed no defect of reason but a deep-seated sense of personal humiliation and injustice that was projected into an extremist cause. A study by Bartlett, Birdwell, and King (2010) contrasting the views of radicals and terrorists suggested that they had different motivations and goals, and that radical views per se did not operate as a gateway to terrorism. Similarly, Meloy and Yakeley (2014) identified that

> … in the final analysis, acts of political violence, terrorism, or civilian massacres … are personal – whether ideologically driven or not – in the sense that an individual decides to commit the act alone or within a closely affiliated group … and the individual's own mind is what differentiates him from the many who are protestors or extremists who do not carry out acts of violence. (p. 348)

This places the explanation firmly within aspects of the individual personality and emotional experience, albeit within a political context. The conclusion of the first author's work in prisons was that an extremist identity met needs for identity, meaning, belonging, safety, respect and status for those who had experienced personal humiliation, alienation, injustice and/or identity confusion and who harboured a deep sense of grievance. In psychoanalytic terms it allows a *good self* to be constructed and maintained through the construction and maintenance of a *bad other.* This defensive splitting involves regression to a simple internal world of good and bad objects rather than whole objects with good and bad qualities (Kernberg, 1976).

Although not formally assessed there were elements of personality disorder in many of those convicted of terrorist offences. Most had accomplished an extreme version of in-group/out-group splitting between the worthy and the unworthy, or the righteous and the unrighteous that is an element of both paranoid and narcissistic personality disorders. The over-idealisation of the in-group and devaluation of the out-group is a feature of borderline personality disorder, and the uncritical acceptance of the authority of a leader by their followers is consistent with dependent personality disorder. Those with a criminal history also evidenced features of antisocial personality disorder such as self-centredness, sensation-seeking, exploitation and disregard for others, underpinned by attitudes that justified violence; all characteristics that were consistent with anti-authority ideologies and that could usefully be deployed in a terrorist cause.

Psychoanalytic understanding

Psychoanalysis has always focused on the underlying causes of violence and aggression. Many psychoanalytical ideas about trauma and violence are relevant to the study of terrorism, especially in connection with individual and group identity. There are several useful psychoanalytical insights about the unconscious motivation for such violence which include trauma, loss, shame and annihilation anxiety. Early experiences that are not digested get replayed when triggered by a new trauma, injustice or insult to oneself, family or ethnic group. Terrorism is a potentially meaningful communication and may be a re-enactment of early trauma as well as a splitting off of the uncomfortable and painful parts of the self and locating them in others.

Terrorism has preoccupied many psychoanalysts and group analysts since Freud. More recently, De Zulueta (2006) has stressed that dehumanisation of the enemy is the result of allowing the dehumanised self to be projected on to the 'other'. Akhtar (2002) quoting Volkan (1997) writes that most major players in a terrorist organisation are themselves deeply traumatised individuals who, as children suffered chronic physical abuse and profound humiliation. Akhtar (2002) claims that the terrorist leader appeals to group members' infantile hunger for love and acceptance in offering what is, in effect a new family with himself in the role of the good father. Hopper (2017, personal communication) also says that hope is essentially a wish to be heard and understood by a good parental figure. De Zulueta (2006) identifies that a recurring finding in the literature is that 'terrorists' are essentially 'normal' people who experienced a lack of social ties or attachments, and she cites Gilligan's (1996) proposition that the basic cause of violent behaviour is the wish to ward off or eliminate feelings of shame or humiliation and replace them with their opposite, feelings of pride. She argues that the loss of cultural and Islamic pride due to centuries of colonialism and exploitation by both the West and their own leadership has been a powerful source of shame, particularly for young men.

Volkan (1988) describes how the role of large group identity shapes the terrorist's individual identity, arguing that it emerges from shared mental representations of large group history that include historical traumas and triumphs that become the source of both collective pride and shame. These events are unconsciously chosen and ritualised by the group to build cohesion and group identity, differentiating themselves from the enemy. Akhtar (2002) states that then 'feeling itself to be a victim, the group begins to victimise others in an act of externalisation' (p. 91).

Political context

These references to large group history stress the importance of geo-political and social contexts. Becoming a terrorist depends on events that expose an asymmetry of power and locate the individual in a power-poor apparently victimised group. The goal of a terrorist attack is to usurp power from the power-rich group, usually identified as government, and provoke a reaction from them. An overly oppressive response from government can escalate antagonism by exposing a lack of concern for the terrorists' cause and result in a loss of moral authority; a process exemplified in the escalation of conflict between the UK Government and the provisional IRA in Northern Ireland during the Troubles. Alderdice (2005), a psychoanalytical psychiatrist and member of the Alliance party at this time, identifies terrorism as a means of exacting revenge for the humiliations heaped upon the power-poor in Ireland over many generations. He suggests that this dynamic of the power-poor provoking the power-strong into counter-productive pathological reactions is commonly enacted in both the consulting room and on the world stage. Parallels can be drawn with the current wave of Islamist terrorism in the UK where grievance, experienced on both a personal and political level, cathected by apparent current political victimisation and in the absence of sufficient protective influences, can become a driver for terrorism.

Three main types of terrorist

It became clear from the first author's dialogue with terrorist offenders in the UK that despite their common vulnerabilities there were also some differences in terms of what they wanted to achieve and in what they would do to achieve it. At the time this work was done, none of those from the UK wanted to introduce Sharia law into the UK; most wanted to demonstrate against British and American foreign policy in Muslim lands. Some wanted to prepare themselves through attending training camps in the UK to fight in a prophesised 'final holy war', others wanted to help Muslims abroad by travelling to areas of conflict as insurgents. In addition, what each individual would do to achieve his goal also varied. Some were persuaded, particularly if they were thwarted in their goal to fight abroad, to carry out a terrorist act in the UK, but not all were prepared to target civilians; some would first seek out a military or government target and settle for a softer civilian target when this proved difficult. In retrospect, those with the most scruples were those who believed they were fighting a noble cause; criminals had fewer scruples. A smaller number occupy a different space altogether in which their narcissistic needs for power and revenge and the opportunity to fight an imagined 'just war' act as a toxic combination transforming them into sadistic killers.

Many of those who have speculated about typologies of terrorism in the past have identified three main types. Miller (2006) in his overview characterised these as comprising an ideologically-driven leader, a number of acolytes drawn to the group's ideals and a number of opportunists meeting personal motives. Hacker (1976) referred to crusaders, criminals and crazies, and Schmid and de Graaf (1982) to political terrorism, (organised) crime-linked terrorism and pathological (crazy) terrorism. In UK prisons we saw noble cause and criminal types (the Good and the Bad), and those who might legitimately be labelled Ugly can be identified from other sources. This describes a syndrome of grievance fuelled violence that is evident in the backgrounds of school shooters, some terrorist leaders, and some lone-actors: those with fixated and delusional beliefs, grandiose but unstable self-esteem, a sense of entitlement, lack of empathy and delusions of grandeur. It is associated with both extreme violence and pervasive psychopathology.

These three types are not mutually exclusive. Mental health difficulties can be present in both noble cause and criminal groups, though a functional link between mental health and terrorist violence is more discernible in the Ugly category. All three groups find common cause in blaming a power-rich group for their apparent disempowerment and victimisation.

The Good: noble cause

One terrorist offender was a university student when he first encountered Islamist ideology. From a traditional Pakistani family he found it hard to adapt to the freedoms of university life after a family-centred self-contained home life. He felt humiliated by his lack of sophistication in comparison with other students and found solace with other Pakistani students who were preoccupied by the plight of Muslims in the Middle East. Over time they abandoned their studies in favour of seeking evidence for their extremist beliefs, travelling to Pakistan with the intention of joining the struggle in Afghanistan. Frustrated in this they turned their attention to plotting a terrorist offence in the UK. Involvement in this provided him with a noble identity and allowed him to overcome his feelings of humiliation, gave him self-respect, a sense of destiny, a friendship group, and someone to blame for his difficulties.

Roberts and Horgan (2003) have identified that individuals are 'socialised into terrorism' by means of small steps that gradually overcome their initial inhibitions about becoming a terrorist. Push and pull factors eventually reach a tipping point that culminate in the decision to engage with a group, cause or ideology. Push factors among those convicted in the UK were broadly feelings of grievance and humiliation, exclusion, dissonance between host and heritage cultures, and a lack of agency, significance, identity, meaning, belonging and worth. Pull factors were broadly the opportunities to achieve an identity of significance, a way of making sense of the world that projected blame on to others, an opportunity to belong to a closely bonded proxy family, to exact revenge, to escape from cultural dissonance and perceived second class status; and for some an outlet for their violence and criminality. The experience of excitement, challenge, adventure and in the context of the emergence of the Islamic state, the opportunity for nation building, can also act as pull factors. Jihadi ideology justifies this attitude shift rather than constituting the prime motivation.

In addition to psychological gains engagement also provides moral superiority. As Meloy and Yakeley (2014) observe

> What distinguishes the predatory violence of the terrorist from other cases of instrumental violence is the moral sanctioning of the act. This is superego-driven homicidal aggression wherein the terrorist finds a mandate for his violence: the drive to

> punish those who are judged morally wrong and therefore disgusting, and the wish to establish an ideal state, or state of mind, that has heretofore eluded him. (p. 362)

These push factors are generic and one would expect them to be fairly widespread within diaspora Muslim communities in the West. To understand why extremist violence is not therefore more common it is necessary to understand the role of factors that protect against involvement. Most individuals are protected by a good enough life, positive relationships, secure friendships, adequate self-esteem, hope for their future and/or sufficient knowledge of Islam that they are not entrained by jihadi ideology. But for the few without sufficient protection, conditioning and grooming within a group or online can achieve an attitude shift that finally overcomes their inhibitions against taking action. The presence of in-group/out-group thinking reflects the accomplishment of a clear split between good and bad objects such that the in-group is experienced as good and worthy and the out-group as bad, unworthy and even inhuman, the reason for their difficulties and the source of their humiliation. The process is helped by the underground nature of terrorist plotting that forges close bonds that lock in loyalty and prevent disaffiliation, maintained through threat or force if necessary.

This pathway was taken by those whose motivation was characterised by 'noble cause'. These individuals did not have any conviction history or criminal motivation for their engagement. They became involved as a result of their grievance against the West for their invasion of Muslim lands in Iraq and Afghanistan and the West's apparent support for Israel and the victimisation of Palestinians. It is proposed that at root this grievance was personal, stemming from narcissistic wounds sustained earlier in life and mirrored on the political stage. Alongside idealism, sensitivity to injustice and a firm belief that they could make the world a better place for Muslims, forged their justification for violence.

Some male offenders recalled racial abuse that mirrored the humiliations from the arbitrary abuse of patriarchal power within the family. In Asian and Arabic cultures patriarchal power holds sway and can manifest in violence towards women and children and fraught relationships with fathers, especially in boys who step into their power in adolescence. This splitting into the power-rich and the power-poor therefore becomes a fundamental organising principle for children in these cultures. The work of the psychoanalyst Kobrin (2010) explores the Arabic Muslim culture that denigrates and victimises women in the home, causing the children to experience their early loved mother as a hated object such that their needs and thinking remain infantile and they find it hard to achieve independence. She believes that the terror in Islamic suicide terrorism is displaced murderous rage for the early mother, stemming from the projection of the hatreds developed through the blaming and shaming childrearing practices of their families.

Among those in prison convicted of terrorist offences, a breakdown in relationship with the father was an almost universal background factor, accompanied in many cases by strong feelings of hate and antagonism towards him. Those who espoused Islamist extremism spoke of being able to trump the authority of the father with their allegiance to Allah and the Muslim cause. 'What are you doing for the umma?[2] … I am a better Muslim than you.'

The Bad: criminal

In contrast, about 60% of those in custody at this time had a criminal history, which ran counter to initial assumptions about the political nature of terrorist offending. The link between terrorism and criminality is now widely evidenced, with Carrapico, Irrera, and Tuman (2015) clarifying established links between terrorists and transnational and organised crime at the macro level. The Belgian offenders who undertook the Paris shootings in November 2015 and Brussels airport and metro bombings in March 2016 came from the impoverished, overcrowded and deprived area of Molenbeek in Belgium described by its Mayor as *'a breeding ground for violence'.* For them, no conditioning or grooming was necessary to develop attitudes supportive of offending; they already had them, as well as polarised beliefs dividing the world into 'Us and Them' or criminals and straight-goers, now labelled 'kuffar'.[3] They were able to deploy their criminal capability for apparent moral as well as financial gain, and launder their offending by a righteous affiliation. Involvement met their criminal needs for status, sensation-seeking, dominance, control, violence and revenge against the authorities, and promised redemption. Such offenders had only a superficial engagement with ideology or cause, sufficient only to justify their terrorist offending; their motivation remained essentially opportunistic.

Alderdice (2005), drawing on his political experiences, highlights the difference between those joining paramilitary groups before and after the Good Friday agreement in Northern Ireland. Earlier members saw themselves as taking up a noble cause, often as a response to personal loss or injury and were disparaging of those referred to as 'Ceasefire Soldiers' who joined to benefit from a culture of organised crime that took hold in the wake of the peace agreement, 'using the political cause as a flag of convenience for crude personal material gain' (p. 578).

In custody, terrorist offenders with a criminal background did not adopt ethnic dress, nor display an exaggerated religiosity. Their appearance was westernised; they identified with mainstream criminals and were scornful of those who presented as religious Muslims. In turn, those motivated by 'noble cause' were scornful of those they saw as criminals motivated purely by revenge. One in particular had a violent background and had committed several serious assaults in custody. He was considered to be the leader of a terrorist cell and had been involved in procuring arms for an Islamist terrorist attack, despite not sharing their ideology or aims. Personality assessment identified him as a psychopath, high on dominance, exploitation of others, sensation-seeking and extroversion, as well as alcohol and drug use. His profile was that of a violent and versatile criminal and his motivation purely opportunistic.

The Ugly: pathological narcissism

Baumeister (1997), exploring the causes of 'evil', concludes that one of the basic causes is high but unstable self-esteem, sometimes referred to as insecure grandiosity. He says: 'I propose that violent, evil people tend to be marked by feelings of superiority but also a fear that they will lose their superior position.' (p. 152). Manne (2014) interprets this psychodynamically as the product of split parenting between an under-valuing (or absent) parent and an over-valuing parent that makes it difficult to integrate good and bad aspects of the self, such that the self is taken as the love object. Kobrin (2010) suggests that suicide terrorism among Arab Muslims is a product of a failure to integrate love of the father with love of a mother who is apparently hated by the father, with suicide achieving a longed for fusion. Similarly, Kernberg (2009), in discussing the evidence for the death drive, identifies the unconscious function of self-destructiveness as not simply an urge to destroy the self but also to destroy significant others, be it out of guilt, revenge, envy, or triumph.

The far-right terrorist Breivik (2017), convicted of the murder of 77 people including 69 teenagers in Norway, is an example of this type of narcissistic killer. Eventually diagnosed with narcissistic personality disorder, his father was absent from his life and his mother depressed and unstable, alternately smothering and rejecting him. He cultivated an image of hyper-masculinity and became obsessed with the political left and their support for multi-culturalism and liberal values which he saw as robbing him of his birthright. He believed he was a modern incarnation of the Knights Templar, a 12th-century group of elite warriors during the Christian crusades. Yet as Buruma (2015), the reviewer of his biography, summed up: 'His is a story of family dysfunction, professional and sexual failure, grotesque narcissism and … apocalyptic delusions'.

Another potential example of pathological narcissism is Mohammed Emwazi, otherwise known as Jihadi John. His terrorist trajectory has been widely reported. His role as a guard and torturer for ISIS appeared to act as a 'narcissistic supply' in which he found satisfaction from inflicting pain and humiliation on those he judged to be unworthy. He not only carried out the beheading of eight individual hostages and oversaw the beheadings of 21 Syrian soldiers but he also was filmed doing so in videos released to the whole world, providing further gratification of his narcissistic needs.

Summary and conclusion

This paper suggests that there are three broad pathways into terrorism, though it is not proposed that they are mutually exclusive. It is the case that many of those who take the noble cause pathway are also troubled, as are many of those with a criminal background. Depression and elements of personality disorder and substance misuse are not uncommon in terrorist offenders, as would be expected in those who have struggled to find their place in society. The inclusion of a clinical pathway in this model is for those few individuals, often lone actors, whose involvement is primarily driven by their often idiosyncratic clinical condition.

This pathway model is an attempt to make sense of the empirical situation that confronts us at a time when our collective understanding of terrorist offending is still in its infancy. Until recently there have been few opportunities to apply psychological analysis to those involved, and the prevailing belief has been that this form of violence is the product of rational decision-making in the pursuit of political aims. The UK correctional imperative to reduce future risk has provided a rare window into the subjective experience of those who have committed terrorist offences and provides an opportunity to develop our understanding of the needs that are met by engaging with extremist ideologies, groups or causes.

Far from pathologising terrorist violence this exercise understands terrorist offending as the product of frustrated normal human needs for love, acceptance and reciprocal trust from infancy through to adulthood. Criminality appears to constitute a vulnerability to radicalisation in itself by virtue of its demonisation by mainstream society and a reciprocal desire on the part of criminals for revenge and redemption. Those with higher levels of conventional psychopathology are found within the smaller group of lone actors with idiosyncratic grievances. In contrast, group actors present as hostile and aggrieved but are largely emotionally and cognitively intact, despite elements of personality disorder and accompanying depression.

Psychoanalytic interpretations are helpful in understanding terrorism as a form of communication driven by unassuaged primal fears and existential threats that through primitive mechanisms allow a persecuting group to become the repository for disavowed feelings, and thereby a target for annihilation. Group analytic interpretations also help to explain how large group history shapes ideology and individual identity, maintains group allegiance and sanctions terrorist offending.

Further experience and research may confirm the utility of this pathway model and provide additional clarification of the intersection between psychopathology and terrorism.

Disclosure statement

No potential conflict of interest was reported by the authors.

Funding

This work was part funded by the Centre for Research and Evidence on Security Threats [ESRC Award: ES/N009614/1].

Notes

1. The Terrorism Act 2006.
2. The global Muslim community.
3. Heretic, unworthy.

References

Akhtar, S. (2002). The psychodynamic dimension of terrorism. In C. Covington, P. Williams, J. Arundale, & J. Knox (Eds.), *Terrorism and war: Unconscious dynamics of political violence* (pp. 87–96). London: Karnac Books.

Alderdice, J. T. (2005). Understanding terrorism: The inner world and the outer world. *British Journal of Psychotherapy, 21*, 577–587.

Arendt, H. (1963). *Eichmann in Jerusalem. A report on the banality of evil*. New York, NY: Viking Press.

Bartlett, J., Birdwell, J., & King, M. (2010). *The edge of violence. A radical approach to extremism*. London: Demos.

Baumeister, R. (1997). *Evil. Inside human violence and cruelty*. (p. 152). New York: Henry Holt and Company.

Breivik, A. (2017). Retrieved July 12, 2017, from https://publicintelligence.net/anders-behring-breiviks-complete-manifesto-2083-a-european-declaration-of-independence/

Buruma, I. (2015). *One of us: The story of Anders Breivik and the massacre in Norway by Åsne Seierstad – review*. Retrieved May 22, 2017, from https://www.theguardian.com/books/2015/feb/26/one-of-us-the-story-of-anders-breivik-massacre-norway-asne-seierstad-review

Carrapico, H., Irrera, D., & Tuman, B. (Eds.). (2015). *Criminals and terrorists in partnership: Unholy alliance*. London: Routledge.

Corner, E., & Gill, P. (2015). A false dichotomy? Mental illness and lone-actor terrorism. *Law and Human Behaviour, 39*, 23–34.

Corner, E., Gill, P., & Mason, O. K. (2016). Mental health disorders and the terrorist: A research note probing selection effects and disorder prevalence. *Studies in Conflict & Terrorism, 39*, 1–19.

Crenshaw, M. (1981). The causes of terrorism. *Comparative Politics, 13*, 379–399.

De Zulueta, F. (2006). Terror breeds terrorists. *Medicine, Conflict and Survival, 22*, 13–25.

Gilligan, J. (1996). *Violence: Our deadliest epidemic and its causes*. New York, NY: Grossnet/Putman.

Hacker, F. (1976). *Crusaders, criminals and crazies: Terror and terrorism in our time*. New York, NY: Norton.

Kernberg, O. (1976). *Object relations theory and clinical psychoanalysis*. New York, NY: Jason Aronson.

Kernberg, O. (2009). The concept of the death drive: A clinical perspective. *The International Journal of Psychoanalysis, 90*, 1009–1023.

Kobrin, N. (2010). *The banality of suicide terrorism: The naked truth about the psychology of Islamic suicide bombing*. Washington, DC: Potomac Books Inc.

Manne, A. (2014). *The life of I. The new culture of narcissism*. Carlton: Melbourne University Press.

Meloy, R., & Yakeley, J. (2014). The violent true believer as a lone wolf – psychoanalytic perspectives on terrorism. *Behavioural Sciences & the Law, 32*, 347–365.

Miller, L. (2006). The Terrorist Mind II. Psychopathologies and practical guidelines for investigation. *International Journal of Offender Therapy and Comparative Criminology, 50*, 255–268.

Roberts, K., & Horgan, J. (2003). Risk assessment and the terrorist. *Perspectives on Terrorism, 2*, 3–9.

Schmid, A. P., & de Graaf, A. J. (1982). *Violence as communication: Insurgent terrorism and the western news media*. London: Sage.

Volkan, V. (1988). *The need to have enemies and allies: From clinical practice to international relationships*. Northvale, NJ: Jason Aronson.

Volkan, V. (1997). *Bloodlines: From ethnic pride to ethnic terrorism*. Boulder, CO: West View Press.

Terrorism and mental disorder, and the role of psychiatrists in counter-terrorism in the UK

Jessica Yakeley and Richard Taylor

In this paper, we review the extant research on the links between terrorism and mental disorder in the light of evolving theoretical frameworks and new empirical evidence, examine the role of the psychiatrist in terrorist prevention as detailed in recently published guidance from the Royal College of Psychiatrists in response to government policy and legislation, and explore the contribution of contemporary psychoanalytic perspectives on existing empirical findings characterising the lone-actor terrorist.

Introduction

The psychological makeup of those who commit acts of terrorism, and the motivations that lead them to do so, have been the subject of intense academic enquiry in the past 50 years. Since 9/11 there has been an explosion in the literature on terrorism research, perspectives and explorations from many different fields of study, including criminology, psychology, sociology and cultural studies. Psychiatrists have for the most part remained at the periphery of such investigations, but with growing media and public attention focused on alleged mental illness in terrorist perpetrators, such as in the attack on Bastille Day in Nice, and the government's efforts to involve health care professionals in terrorist prevention, including pressures to develop specific risk assessment tools for terrorists, they are, willingly or unwillingly, pulled into the realm of terrorism studies. Immersion in the world of anti-terrorist activities can be exciting and seductive with its aura of secrecy and high-level contact with 'special' criminal justice agencies. However, psychiatrists may be at risk of straying from their professional duties, working outside of their expertise and overstepping ethical boundaries by engaging with the government's efforts to prevent terrorism.

Historical understanding of mental illness and terrorism

The presence of psychopathology in individual terrorists is one of a range of factors that may play a role in driving them towards terrorist activity. Gill and Corner, two of the most prominent contemporary researchers in the field, offer a helpful overview of the study of the relationship between mental disorder and engagement in terrorism since the 1970s (Corner & Gill, 2015; Gill & Corner, 2017), demonstrating how the pendulum for the explanatory emphasis on mental disorder has swung from centre stage to the periphery and back again.

Psychopathy

The prevailing theory in the 1970s was that terrorism was caused by psychopathy. Writers such as Cooper (1978) proposed that individuals drawn to terrorist activities were those who already showed deviant characteristics and sociopathic behaviour, and terrorist violence provided an outlet for their aggressive impulses. However, these views were influenced by popular culture, lacked objective evidence and lost credibility once the concept of psychopathy was more closely defined by Hare in his empirically based development of the Revised Psychopathy Checklist (PCL-R; Hare, 1991) the most widely validated and used instrument to assess psychopathy.

Psychoanalytic approaches

Although psychopathy became less popular as a causal theory of the terrorist, psychological explanations remained central to the understanding of terrorist activity. Psychoanalytic theory became the prevalent paradigm, focusing on the development of pathological narcissism as being key to the personality of the terrorist. Informed by the influential theories of Kohut (1971) and Kernberg (1984) regarding the aetiology and development of narcissism and narcissistic character disorders, it was postulated that individuals prone to becoming terrorists had experienced emotional deprivation and other traumas in childhood and in an effort to overcome such adversity developed narcissistic defences of grandiosity, contempt for others, denial of attachments and pathological aggression. Such individuals were vulnerable to any threat to their self-esteem and sense of self, and would react with narcissistic rage and violence towards others (Pearlstein, 1991). Terrorist action could therefore be explained by the unconscious displacement of anger towards early parental figures onto others who must be killed for political or religious reasons. These theories were backed up by some empirical studies, such as that of a German extremist movement in which 250 cases of terrorism were interviewed and analysed (Jager, Schmidtchen, & Sullwold, 1981). This showed that a quarter to a third of the sample had experienced parental loss, parental conflict and abuse in childhood, but the study was later criticised for its poor methodology (Victoroff, 2005).

Terrorism is not caused by mental illness

The association between mental disorder and terrorism was downplayed, stemming from researchers highlighting the lack of empirical evidence to support these psychoanalytic explanations. An accumulating range of studies suggested terrorists were more likely to be psychologically normal (Borum, 2004; Horgan, 2005; Silke, 1998; Victoroff, 2005). This shift in explanatory paradigm was in part influenced by a greater interest in the role of group dynamics in determining terrorist motivation, based on research within terrorist groups in different parts of the world, such as the Irish Republican Army (IRA), Hezbollah, Colombian terrorists and Palestinian jihadists, that showed the recruits were mostly absent of psychopathology. This observation was explained by terrorist organisations needing psychologically healthy individuals who were capable of carrying out terrorist activities that required calculated violence and the need for secrecy, as well as the ability to work effectively with others within the terrorist cell. Psychologically damaged people, including those with mental illness, would pose a liability to the effective functioning of terrorist groups and would be weeded out in the selection process. However, these researchers did not deny the presence of pathological disorders altogether in terrorists, but highlighted that the prevalence of various mental disorders was the same as that of the normal population. These views led to a dramatic shift in attributing terrorist activity to mental dysfunctions in individual terrorists to the opposing assertion, backed by a proliferation of the literature that there was no association whatsoever between mental disorder and terrorism (Horgan, 2003; Silke, 2003; Victoroff, 2005).

Critical evaluation

Gill and Corner (2017) have critically evaluated the aforementioned studies dismissing the link between mental disorder and terrorism by highlighting an erroneous conflation of mental illness and rationality; a lack of differentiation between different types of terrorists, particularly between group terrorists and those acting alone; and a lack of specificity in their generalisations of pathology under the rubrics of mental illness, mental disorder, psychopathology or psychopathy, without specifying actual clinical diagnoses which could range from the more mild such as anxiety and depression, to the more extreme in cases of psychosis.

We would also suggest that other factors have influenced the rebuttal of the idea that mental disorder has anything to do with terrorism. First, such a view may be politically unacceptable in being seen as sympathising with the terrorist and letting them evade responsibility. This stance is exemplified in the case of Francisco Martin Duran who was convicted of attempting to assassinate former president of the United States, Bill Clinton, in 1994. The U.S. Attorney Eric Holder stated; 'Very often in society, people try to use excuses to deflect responsibility.' Secondly, political and religious themes are among the commonest delusions in paranoid psychotic illnesses but may be mistaken for justifiable and rational beliefs of a sane person, rather than being the result of psychotic processes. This was illustrated in a study of 24 lone perpetrators who carried out serious, and in some cases fatal, attacks on European politicians between 1990 and 2004, in which a high proportion of the attackers were found to be psychotic, but their delusional fixations on these public figures had been mistaken for politically motivated beliefs (James et al., 2007).

Finally, there has been a lack of differentiation in the literature between mental illness and personality disorder. The term mental disorder is often equated with mental illness, rather than being a category that also includes personality disorder, and hence the latter is not formally diagnosed, and/or the presence of abnormal personality traits is missed or ignored. This confusion may be particularly evident where the terrorist exhibits disturbed and entrenched states of mind such as grievance, and it is not clear whether such thinking is on the extreme end of the spectrum of normality, due to delusional thinking, or is the manifestation of a personality disorder. Moreover, the diagnosis of narcissistic personality disorder may be missed by UK psychiatrists being unfamiliar with the DSM-5 diagnostic criteria (American Psychiatric Association, 2013) as it does not appear as a separate personality disorder in the ICD-10 (World Health Organisation (WHO), 1992), the classification system which most psychiatrists in the UK are more familiar with. Such nosological controversies were played out between the psychiatrists evaluating Anders Breivik, the Norwegian far-right terrorist who killed 77 people in Norway in 2011. The psychiatrists were split between those who asserted he was suffering from a psychotic illness and those who diagnosed him with a severe personality disorder.

Contemporary research

Terrorist trajectories

The current field of terrorist research offers a more balanced and nuanced approach to the study of the link between mental disorder and terrorism, recognising its complexity and multi-factorial nature, and different stages in the trajectory of terrorist involvement. Thus Horgan (2008) outlines three phases: becoming involved, being involved and disengaging, each phase having different relationships to mental disorder. This model challenges the assumption that mental disorder might cause terrorist activity, by suggesting the reverse – that involvement in terrorism may result in mental disorder, which may not have been present prior to this involvement. The second author, RT, was involved in a study in the UK (Robbins et al., 2005) that showed evidence of mental illness, particularly clinical depression, post-traumatic stress disorder and psychosis, in a number of foreign nationals detained indefinitely under the Anti-Terrorism Crime and Security Act 2001 as being a threat to national security, and concluded that detention per se was likely to be the causative factor to these psychiatric illnesses rather than pre-existing psychopathology. The detainees' deterioration in mental health was explained as a result of various factors intrinsic to their current situation, including their mistrust of the prison regime, a failure in the perception of prison staff in their perception of self-harm and distressed behaviour as being due to mental distress rather than manipulative behaviour, and the psychological impact of not knowing if and when they would be released. Moreover, mental illness and psychological distress may motivate disengagement from terrorist groups. Although to date there is limited evidence for this theory, many deradicalisation programmes in conflict zones such as Saudi Arabia, Singapore and the Middle East, offer psychological interventions with some success. The first author (JY) is currently involved in work at the Tavistock and Portman NHS Foundation Trust commissioned by the Home Office, offering assessments and therapeutic interventions for radicalised British nationals returning from Syria.

The lone actor

More recently, different subtypes of terrorist have been recognised, for example the lone-actor, the suicide bomber and the freedom fighter. One of the most significant research discoveries regarding mental disorder and terrorism to emerge in recent years is that the prevalence of mental disorder may differ between group and lone-actor terrorists. Lone actor or 'lone wolf' terrorist behaviour has been defined by Simon (2013, p. 38) as: 'the use or threat of violence or non-violent sabotage by an individual acting alone, or with minimal support from one or two other people, to further a political, social, religious, financial or other related goal, or, when not having such an objective nevertheless has the same effect upon government and society in terms of creating fear and/or disrupting daily life and/or causing government and society to react with heightened security and/or other responses'. Several studies have found higher rates of mental disorder in lone actors compared with matched samples of group actors (Corner & Gill, 2015; Gruenewald, Chermak, & Freilich, 2013; Merari, Diamant, Bibi, Broshi, & Zakin, 2010a; Merari et al., 2010b). Corner and Gill's study was based on the largest samples of terrorists, comparing 119 lone-actor terrorists with 428 group-based actors, and found that 41% of the lone-based actors had a history of mental health problems and were 13.5 times more likely to have a history of mental illness than group-based terrorists. Those lone actors with mental illness were more likely to have a spouse or partner who was involved in a wider movement, more likely to have been a recent victim of prejudice, and more likely to have experienced recent and chronic stress. They were also more likely to be wedded to a single-issue ideology rather than Al-Qaeda or extreme right-wing ideologies, and to be fixated on a target that they held solely responsible for their grievance.

The suicide bomber

There is also emerging evidence which challenges the traditional view that suicide terrorists are not truly suicidal but motivated by a selfless commitment to their cause, rather than a desire to end their lives. Merari (2010) conducted direct clinical interviews with a sample of Palestinian suicide terrorists, a control group of non-suicide terrorists and a group of organisers of suicide attacks. They found that the would-be suicides had a significantly lower level of ego strength than the organisers of martyrdom attacks, and were more likely to exhibit impulsive and emotionally unstable personality traits, or a dependent and avoidant personality style that made them more susceptible to group, leader and public influence. Some of the potential suicide bombers, but none of the control and organisers groups' participants displayed sub-clinical suicidal tendencies, and significantly more martyr than control group members displayed symptoms of depression.

Interesting gender differences in the motivations and recruitment of suicide bombers have also been documented, which may suggest differences in prevalence rates of mental disorder between male and female bombers. Jacques and Taylor (2008) coded biographical accounts of 30 female and 30 male suicide terrorists for method of recruitment, motivation for attack and outcome of attack. The sample was comprised of suicide bombers involved in terrorism in a number of different areas and organisations: for the women, the Middle East (including operatives of Fatah's Tanzim, the Al-Asqa Brigade, Hamas, and the Palestinian Islamic Jihad); Chechen separatists; The Liberation Tigers of Tamil Eelam (LTTE) and Al Qaeda; for the men, the Middle East, Al Qaeda; separatist groups in Pakistan and Kurdistan and the LTTE. A log-linear analysis found that female suicide terrorists were motivated more by personal events, whereas males were motivated more by religious/nationalistic factors. Females were equally likely as males to be recruited through peer influence, exploitation or self promotion, whereas males were more likely to be recruited as a result of religious persuasion. The types of personal events coded in females included a history of drug problems, and stated wishes to end their lives with a prior history of drug overdose and self-reported depression suggesting the presence of mental disorder in some of these suicide bombers which were more common in women than men.

Diagnoses

Finally, the false dichotomy of single diagnosis (usually psychotic) mentally ill terrorist vs. non-mentally ill terrorist, based on binary thinking and narrow, linear explanations, has been challenged. More recent studies have looked at the full range of psychopathology that may be present in terrorist samples to investigate which diagnostic mental disorders are more common and which are less common. In Corner, Gill, and Mason's (2016) sample of lone-actor terrorists, three disorders had a higher prevalence than in the general population – schizophrenia, delusional disorder and autistic spectrum disorders – and three disorders exhibited a lower prevalence – depression, sleep disorders and learning disabilities.

We would suggest, however, that Corner and Gill's research presents several limitations, in that it is based on the study of publicly available records (court, police, media) rather than conducting clinical interviews; that some of the perpetrators studied were dead; and that the researchers are political scientists not psychiatrists or other mental health clinicians. Nevertheless, their research is important in shifting the emphasis from monocausal explanations (e.g. mental disorder causes terrorist activity in some individuals) to a multifactorial model in which mental disorder is one risk factor that, with other risk factors, may lead to radicalisation and becoming a terrorist.

Re-evaluating psychoanalytic approaches to terrorism research

Persuaded by assertions that there was no hard scientific evidence for the psychoanalytic theories of the mind and motivations of the terrorist, psychoanalytic thinking has for the most part been ignored or dismissed by psychiatrists currently involved in the field of terrorism in the UK and the US. However, the burgeoning accumulation of studies exploring mental illness and terrorism in the past 15 years has been paralleled by a growing body of literature offering a psychoanalytic perspective on terrorism, which incorporates the work of psychiatrists in the field who have had direct contact with terrorists. Most prominent among these are Post (2007) in his work with Palestinian freedom fighters and Alderdice (2005) in his work with Northern Irish terrorists.

Violence as communication

There are three main themes that emerge from the psychoanalytic literature on terrorism (Meloy & Yakeley, 2014). The first is that the terrorist act, as with any violent behaviour, can be understood as an unconscious communication of feelings that cannot be tolerated or put into words but are expelled through bodily action – the maiming or extermination of the body of others, and in the case of the suicide bomber, the annihilation of the body of the terrorist himself. The overt political or religious message inherent in the terrorist's violent action may conceal a constellation of unconscious psychic processes – conflicts, traumatic memories, fantasies, wishes and defences, that may stem from early traumas and adverse experiences but whose meaning remains unconscious.

Transgenerational trauma

The second theme is that of transgenerational traumas: how terrorist activities may be a repetition and re-enactment of historical conflicts and traumas which may go back many generations, and that threaten the identity of the group or society in which the terrorist(s) belongs. This is an example of Freud's (1920) repetition compulsion – that if past traumas remain unresolved, unspoken and not understood, they will be repeated and perpetuated in a vicious cycle of violence. For example, the rise of terrorism in the Palestinians may be linked to historical traumatic and humiliating experiences of being subjugated by Western countries. Alderdice (2005) highlights how experiences of disrespect and humiliation may drive violence as a revenge for social and cultural wrongs perpetrated by others and the need to reverse the experience of humiliation that has been inflicted.

Group identity

The third theme is the role of group forces and dynamics in understanding how large group identities influence and intersect with the identity of the individual terrorist (Volkan, 1988). The identity of any group is shaped by the shared current and historical experiences of the individuals within it. Where these are characterised by collective traumas, losses and experiences of shame and humiliation as described above, these may be chosen to strengthen group cohesion around national, ethnic, cultural or religious identities, and to distinguish the group from the enemy. Moreover, group dynamics act to foster regression in the group's component members from higher mental functioning and rational thought to more primitive mental states in which powerful emotions and impulses govern, and any capacity for reflection and tolerance of others who may be different is lost. Primitive affects and defences dominate – feelings of hatred, contempt, shame and humiliation are projected into others via violent behaviour, and there is idealisation of the group to which they belong, and denigration of others.

Psychoanalytic contributions to risk assessment

A psychoanalytic model incorporating these ideas may be useful in offering a lens through which existing empirical evidence can be reviewed to gain a greater understanding of the mind of the terrorist, the structure and dynamics of his internal world, and the motivations and triggers for his violent actions.

Meloy, a psychoanalytically informed forensic psychologist in the US, has extensively studied the existing empirical research on terrorism, and with his own experience of assessing lone terrorists over the past 20 years and work for the Federal Bureau of Investigation (FBI) and other US Government agencies, has identified 8 proximal warning behaviours and 10 distal characteristics of the lone terrorist, which have been validated in a number of studies including Gill's large sample of lone-actor terrorists in Europe and the US (Meloy & Gill, 2016). The 10 characteristics that he found were most likely to be present in the lone terrorist were the following: personal grievance and moral outrage; the framing of an ideology; failure to affiliate with an extremist group; dependence on a virtual community found on the Internet; the thwarting of occupational goals; radicalisation fuelled by changes in thinking and emotion — including cognitive rigidity, clandestine excitement, contempt and disgust — regardless of the particular ideology; the failure of sexual pair bonding and the sexualisation of violence; greater creativity and innovation than terrorist groups; predatory violence sanctioned by moral (superego) authority; and mental disorder.

Meloy and Yakeley (2014) suggest that these characteristics of the lone-actor terrorist can be helpfully formulated within a psychoanalytically informed object relational framework to provide a more detailed description of, and meaning to, his psychic functioning, intra- and inter-personal relationships, and actions. They postulate that the mind of the lone terrorist is predicated on a pathological narcissistic organisation, sustained by grandiose and omnipotent fantasies, and in which early, pre-oedipal affects and defences predominate. Primitive and self-focused emotions of shame, excitement, envy, rage, contempt, and disgust govern, and more mature affects, such as guilt, remorse, fear and empathy, which require appreciation of a whole object and are necessary for meaningful object relating, are lacking. By contrast, the internal world is populated by part-object relationships and governed by early defence mechanisms such as splitting, denial, omnipotence and projection, and there is a lack of more mature defence mechanisms such as repression and sublimation. The lone wolf's conscious rationalisation of his moral or ideological beliefs may be based on the unconscious projection of personal grievance that defends against deficits in his superego functioning, and in some cases against psychotic decompensation. The latter may manifest as a diagnosable psychotic illness, but it may be more helpful to adopt a more dimensional approach to what is seen as the terrorist's mental disorder, by focusing on his mental structure and psychological processes manifest in the psychodynamic distortions and disturbances in his cognitions, ideations, fantasies, affects, ego defence mechanisms, object relating, superego functioning and impulse control.

These findings have informed the development of a structured clinical risk assessment tool, the Terrorist Radicalization Assessment Protocol-18 (TRAP-18) (Meloy & Gill, 2016). Although psychoanalytic approaches to risk assessment are well documented (e.g. Doctor, 2004) and practically used within mental health services (Kirtchuk, Reiss, & Gordon, 2008), this is the first psychoanalytically informed instrument that has been specifically designed for the assessment of terrorism risk.

The Prevent Strategy

In 2003, the UK Home Office introduced the UK's counter-terrorism strategy, CONTEST, which was revised in 2006, 2009 and most recently 2011 (HM Government, 2011a). It is divided into four work streams: Pursue – the investigation and disruption of terrorism attacks; Prevent – work to stop people becoming terrorists or supporting terrorism; Protect – improving protective security to stop a terrorist attack; and Prepare – working to minimise the impact of an attack and to recover as quickly as possible. Channel, a key part of the Prevent Strategy, is a multi-agency programme focusing on the identification of individuals at risk of being drawn into terrorism and providing them with support (HM Government, 2015).

Channel has developed a Vulnerability Assessment Framework to guide decisions about whether an individual needs support to address their vulnerability to radicalisation and the kind of support that they need (HM Government, 2012).

The Prevent Strategy (HM Government, 2011b) has provoked the most controversy of the four CONTEST work streams, particularly in its relationship to the Muslim community. There has been considerable concern that it has stigmatised and alienated Muslims and legitimised and reinforced Islamophobia, and that its purpose is to discipline Muslim communities, or domesticate British Islam, by constituting Muslims as a 'suspect community' (Pantazis & Pemberton, 2009). It may also provoke dissent and paranoia within the Muslim community by encouraging intelligence gathering within communities. Moreover, the process of identifying potential terrorists is not based on sufficient empirical evidence and there are many accounts of individuals who have been unjustly referred to the Channel programme, causing unwarranted distress for both them and their families.

Prevent's relationship with the health care profession has been equally vexed. Section 26 (1) of the Counter-Terrorism and Security Act 2015 states that specified authorities, including health bodies, 'must, in the exercise of their functions, have due regard to the need to prevent people from being drawn into terrorism'. This has been referred to as the Prevent duty, and has resulted in Prevent training, which has been rolled out across the National Health Service (HM Government, 2016). NHS England has incorporated Prevent into its safeguarding arrangements, so that Prevent awareness and other relevant training are delivered to all staff who provide services to NHS patients. Since April 2013 commissioners have used the Safeguarding section of the NHS Standard Contract to require all NHS trusts to embed Prevent into their delivery of services, policies and training. The intercollegiate guidance, *Safeguarding children and Young people: roles and competences for health care staff* (Royal College of Paediatrics & Child Health, 2014) includes Prevent information and identifies competencies for all health care staff against six levels. Providers are expected to have in place a programme to deliver Prevent training, resourced with accredited facilitators; processes in place to ensure that staff receive Prevent awareness training appropriate to their role; and procedures to comply with the Prevent Training and Competencies Framework. Local safeguarding forums, including local commissioners and providers of NHS Services have oversight of fulfilling the duty and ensuring effective delivery.

The role of psychiatrists in counter-terrorism

The role of the psychiatric profession in the prevention of terrorism has been hotly debated. There is concern that psychiatrists will be put in the role of agents of the state who are expected to prioritise public protection over the individual welfare of patients, and that the identification and monitoring of those suspected at risk of radicalisation may interfere with professional judgement regarding the clinical diagnosis of mental disorder and treatment. The development of risk assessment tools designed to single out potential terrorists have not only raised ethical questions over their use but have also been criticised for their validity and reliability and the lack of empirical research investigating their utility.

In 2016, the Royal College of Psychiatrists issued guidelines regarding the role of psychiatry in counter-terrorism (Royal College of Psychiatrists, 2016). Psychiatrists may have contact with patients suspected of terrorist involvement in a variety of settings, such as prisons and young offender institutions, secure and youth patient forensic services, immigration detention centres, court diversion schemes or acting as an expert witness to provide medico-legal reports to the courts. However, the burden of mandated terrorism detection does not solely fall upon forensic psychiatry: all psychiatrists may encounter patients in whom the seeds of radicalisation and temptation towards terrorist activities might be construed as flourishing. Child and adolescent psychiatrists are particularly in the limelight in being expected, as with the teaching profession, to spot children and young people who may be vulnerable to being radicalised.

This guidance highlights the various ethical dilemmas psychiatrists may encounter in their duty to comply with the Prevent Strategy.

Confidentiality and disclosure

The risk that engagement with Prevent may breach patient confidentiality has provoked the most concern. All doctors must place the care, treatment and safety of their patients at the centre of their work and this includes protecting the patient's confidentiality. Any information sharing or disclosure needs to be considered within the framework of the existing professional guidance on confidentiality and disclosure from the Royal College of Psychiatrists (2010); General Medical Council (GMC, 2017); and the Department of Health (2003, 2010). The GMC has been clear that the Prevent Duty does not impose new duties on doctors or alter the circumstances in which doctors are obliged to report concerns about patients. Psychiatrists should not be urged to act against their best-evidenced clinical judgement. This may be particularly pertinent to those working in relative isolation from peers in criminal justice settings such as police cells, prisons and the courts, who may be subject to overt or subtle pressures to stray beyond their professional remit, such as advising on 'profiling'. Psychiatrists may also be drawn into the seductive qualities of 'secret' work, which risks compromising their clinical professionalism. Concern has also been voiced about pressure on psychiatrists to refer patients to Channel if they see signs of socialisation into extremist thought or groups, without evidence of exploitation or current plans to harm. Unnecessary disclosures will disrupt therapeutic relationships with patients, or deter people from using mental health services at all.

Stigma

Linking mental health with violent radicalisation increases the stigma that is already associated with mental illness. Such an association, that may be promulgated by the media, reinforces commonly held beliefs that mentally ill people are prone to enacting unpredictable and dangerous behaviour which puts others at risk, and will inhibit people with psychological distress and mental disorders from seeking help and accessing treatment. Tackling stigma and discrimination is a key priority of the Royal College of Psychiatrists and other mental health organisations, and all psychiatrists should be mindful of the risk that implementing the Prevent duty may undermine progress in this area.

Risk assessment tools

There have been a number of structured risk assessment tools that have been developed in the last few years. These include the Violent Extremist Risk Assessment (VERA; Pressman, 2009), modelled after the HCR-20 (Douglas, Hart, Webster, & Belfrage, 2013), the Multi-level Guidelines for the Assessment and Management of Group-Based Violence (MLG; Cook, Hart, & Kropp, 2013); the Extremism Risk Guidelines (ERG 22+; HM Government, 2011c; Lloyd & Dean, 2015) and the Terrorism Radicalization Assessment Protocol (TRAP-18; Meloy & Gill, 2016) mentioned above. However, there remain central conceptual and methodological challenges in the development of these instruments (Monahan, 2012). The epidemiological database essential to construct a valid risk-assessment instrument is limited, the base-rates for radicalisation or for preparation of terrorist acts are unknown, and it is unlikely that an instrument to assess the risk of terrorism can be validated prospectively. Many of the known risk factors for common violence are not risk factors for violent terrorism, so that current instruments used to assess the risk of non-terrorist violence cannot be simply adapted into instruments to assess the risk of terrorist violence. The College guidance recommends that risk assessments are best conducted on a case-by-case basis as part of professional safeguarding practices.

Conclusion

With the prospect of terrorism becoming a daily part of our lives, work on counter-terrorism continues apace with the development of more sophisticated methods of profiling and identifying terrorist actors, and ascertaining their motivations and triggers to violence, and the implementation of effective prevention strategies. As psychiatrists ourselves, we believe that the psychiatric profession does have a part to play in counter-terrorism via thoughtful engagement with the Government's Prevent policy, its training and the potential identification of individuals at risk. Psychiatrists should also have some knowledge of the evolving research into the relationship between mental disorder and acts of terrorism, and to be open to different epistemological approaches to the subject that may be seen as complimentary rather than mutually exclusive. However, our primary responsibility remains protecting the best interests of our patients, and we must not be pulled into a territory that falls outside of our areas of expertise or ethical boundaries. Responding to terrorist attacks requires rapid decisions and action; however, optimal clinical care stems from a cautious and considered approach based on our understanding and compassion that has built up over time within the therapeutic relationship.

Disclosure statement

No potential conflict of interest was reported by the authors.

References

Alderdice, J. L. (2005). Understanding terrorism: The inner world and the wider world. *British Journal of Psychotherapy, 21*, 577–587.

American Psychiatric Association. (2013). *Diagnostic and statistical manual of mental disorders* (5th ed.). Washington, DC.

Borum, R. (2004). *Psychology of terrorism.* Tampa, FL: University of South Florida Tampa Department of Mental Health Law and Policy.

Cook, A., Hart, S., & Kropp, R. (2013). *Multi-level guidelines for the assessment and management of group-based violence.* Burnaby: Mental Health, Law, and Policy Institute, Simon Fraser University.

Cooper, H. H. A. (1978). Terrorist as psychopath. *Legal Medical Quarterly, 2*, 253–262.

Corner, E., & Gill, P. (2015). A false dichotomy? Mental illness and lone-actor terrorism. *Law and Human Behavior,* 39, 23–34.

Corner, E., Gill, P., & Mason, O. (2016). Mental health disorders and the terrorist: A research note probing selection effects and disorder prevalence. *Studies in Conflict & Terrorism, 39*, 560–568.

Department of Health. (2003). *NHS Code of Practice on Confidentiality.* London.

Department of Health. (2010). *Supplementary Guidance on Public Interest Disclosures.* London.

Doctor, R. (2004). Psychodynamic lessons in risk assessment and management. *Advances in Psychiatric Treatment, 10*, 267–276.

Douglas, K., Hart, S., Webster, C., & Belfrage, H. (2013). *The HCR-20 V3. Assessing risk for violence user guide.* Burnaby: Mental Health, Law, and Policy Institute, Simon Fraser University.

General Medical Council. (2017). *Confidentiality.* London.

Gill, P., & Corner, E. (2017). There and back again: The study of mental disorder and terrorist involvement. *American Psychologist,* 72: 231–241.

Gill, P., Horgan, J., Corner, E., & Silver, J. (2016). Indicators of lone actor violent events: The problems of low base rates and long observational periods. *Journal of Threat Assessment and Management, 3*, 165–173.

Gruenewald, J., Chermak, S., & Freilich, J. D. (2013). Distinguishing 'Loner' attacks from other domestic extremist violence: A comparison of far-right homicide incident and offender characteristics. *Criminology & Public Policy,* 12: 65–91.

Hare, R. (1991). *Manual of the Revised Psychopathy Checklist.* Toronto: Multi Health Systems.

HM Government. (2011a). *CONTEST: The United Kingdom's strategy for countering terrorism.* London: TSO (The Stationery Office).

HM Government. (2011b). *Prevent Strategy.* London: TSO (The Stationery Office).

HM Government. (2011c). *Extremism risk guidelines: ERG 22+ structured professional guidelines for assessing risk of extremist offending.* London: National Offender Management Service.

HM Government. (2012). *Channel: Vulnerability assessment framework.* London: TSO (The Stationery Office).

HM Government. (2015). *Channel duty guidance: Protecting vulnerable people from being drawn into terrorism.* London: TSO (The Stationery Office).

HM Government. (2016) *Prevent: Training Catalogue.* London: TSO (The Stationery Office).

Horgan, J. (2003). The search for the terrorist. In A. Silke (Ed.), *Terrorists, victims and society: Psychological perspectives on terrorism and its consequences* (pp. 3–27). Chichester, England: Wiley.

Horgan, J. (2005). *The psychology of terrorism.* London: Routledge.

Horgan, J. H. (2008). From profiles to pathways and roots to routes: Perspectives from psychology on radicalization into terrorism. *Annals of the American Academy of Political and Social Science, 618*, 80–94.

Jacques, K., & Taylor, P. J. (2008). Male and female suicide bombers: Different sexes, different reasons? *Studies in Conflict & Terrorism, 31*, 304–326.

Jager, H., Schmidtchen, G., & Sullwold, L. (1981). *Lebenslaufanalysen.* (Vol. 2). Opladen: Westdeutscher Verlag.

James, D. V., Mullen, P. E., Meloy, J. R., Pathé, M. T., Farnham, F. R., Preston, L., & Darnley, B. (2007). The role of mental disorder in attacks on European politicians 1990–2004. *Acta Psychiatrica Scandinavica, 116*, 334–344.

Kernberg, O. F. (1984). *Severe Personality Disorders.* Yale University Press.

Kirtchuk, G., Reiss, D., & Gordon, J. (2008). Interpersonal dynamics in the everyday practice of a forensic unit. *Psychic assaults and frightened clinicians: Countertransference in forensic settings.* London: Karnac Books. 97–112.

Kohut, H. (1971). *The analysis of the self.* New York, NY: International Universities Press.

Lloyd, M., & Dean, C. (2015). The development of structured guidelines for assessing risk in extremist offenders. *Journal of Threat Assessment and Management,* 2, 40–52.

Meloy, J. R., & Gill, P. (2016). The lone-actor terrorist and the TRAP-18. *Journal of Threat Assessment and Management, 3*, 37–52.

Meloy, J. R., & Yakeley, J. (2014). The violent true believer as a 'Lone Wolf' – Psychoanalytic perspectives on terrorism. *Behavioral Sciences & the Law, 32*, 347–365.

Merari, A. (2010). *Driven to death: Psychological and social aspects of suicide terrorism.* Oxford: Oxford University Press.

Merari, A., Diamant, I., Bibi, A., Broshi, Y., & Zakin, G. (2010a). Personality characteristics of 'self martyrs'/'suicide bombers' and organizers of suicide attacks. *Terrorism and Political Violence, 22*, 87–101.

Merari, A., Fighel, J., Ganor, B., Lavie, E., Tzoreff, Y., & Livne, A. (2010b). Making Palestinian 'martyrdom operations'/'suicide attacks': Interviews with would-be perpetrators and organizers. *Terrorism and Political Violence, 22*, 102–119.

Monahan, J. (2012). The individual risk assessment of terrorism. *Psychology, Public Policy, and Law, 18*, 167–205.

Pantazis, C., & Pemberton, S. (2009). From the 'Old' to the 'New' suspect community: Examining the impacts of recent UK counter–terrorist legislation. *British Journal of Criminology, 49*, 646–666.

Pearlstein, R. M. (1991). *The mind of the political terrorist.* Wilmington: Scholarly Resources.

Post, J. M. (2007). *The mind of the terrorist*. New York, NY: Palgrave Macmillan.

Pressman, D. E. (2009). *Risk assessment decisions for violent political extremism 2009–02*. Ottawa: Public Safety Canada.

Robbins, I., MacKeith, J., Davison, S., Kopelman, M., Meux, C., Ratnam, S., … Taylor, R. (2005). Psychiatric problems of detainees under the Anti-Terrorism Crime and Security Act 2001. *Psychiatric Bulletin, 29*, 407–409.

Royal College of Paediatrics and Child Health. (2014). *Safeguarding Children and Young people: Roles and competences for health care staff*. London: RCPCH. www.rcpch.ac.uk/sites/default/files/page/SafeguardingChildren

Royal College of Psychiatrists. (2010). *Good Psychiatric Practice: Confidentiality and Information Sharing (CR160)*. London: Royal College of Psychiatrists.

Royal College of Psychiatrists (2016). *Counter-terrorism and psychiatry. Position Statement PS04/16*. London: Royal College of Psychiatrists.

Silke, A. (1998). Cheshire-cat logic: The recurring theme of terrorist abnormality in psychological research. *Psychology, Crime & Law, 4*, 51–69.

Silke, A. (2003). Becoming a terrorist. In A. Silke (Ed.), *Terrorists, victims and society: Psychological perspectives on terrorism and its consequences* (pp. 29–53). Chichester: Wiley.

Simon, J. D. (2013). *Lone wolf terrorism*. Amherst, NY: Prometheus Books.

Victoroff, J. (2005). The mind of the terrorist: A review and critique of psychological approaches. *Journal of Conflict Resolution, 49*, 3–42.

Volkan, V. D. (1988). *The need to have enemies and allies: From clinical practice to international relationships*. Northvale, NJ: Jason Aronson.

World Health Organisation (WHO). (1992). *International Classification of Mental and Behavioural Disorders, Tenth Edition (ICD-10)*. Geneva: WHO.

Working together to break the 'circles of fear' between Muslim communities and mental health services

Angela Byrne, Shirin Mustafa and Imam Qamruzzaman Miah

This article discusses the risks posed to the relationships between Muslim communities and mental health services by the current focus on radicalisation. We employ the 'Circles of Fear' formulation to understand these risks and describe how we are working to break these circles of fear in our work with communities in Tower Hamlets, East London.

In 2002, an influential report for the Sainsbury Centre for mental health identified 'circles of fear' in the relationships between African and Caribbean communities and mental health services (Keating, Robertson, McCulloch, & Frances, 2002). The review which led to this proposal was conducted in the context of the ongoing over-representation of African and Caribbean communities in mental health services and poorer outcomes and adverse experiences compared to white communities and with the recognition that there needed to be change within mental health services to address the entrenched relationships of mistrust.

This formulation proposes that relationships between African and Caribbean communities and mental health services are characterised by 'circles of fear' in which African and Caribbean people mistrust or fear mental health services and service providers fear Black service users and also fear talking about issues of 'race' and culture. Thus, people tend to avoid mental health services until times of crisis when they are more likely to be admitted through aversive pathways and experience coercive treatment, which may be driven by fear and racist stereotypes and so a negative spiral is created and entrenched.

Within this approach, the origins of fear include aversive pathways into services, especially where mental health services are seen as being linked to coercive agencies such as the police and prisons (Keating & Robertson, 2004) as well as adverse experiences within services, such as over-use of medication, restraint and isolation. An important driver of this is the process of 'othering' communities, seeing them as a threat, as well as ignorance, racism and stereotypes, such as 'big, black and dangerous' (Prins, Backer-Holst, Francis, & Keitch, 1993; cited in Keating et al., 2002, p. 26) which is linked to the coercive control described above.

Sadly, this formulation is as pertinent today as it was in 2002. The problem of over-representation has not gone away (e.g. Care Quality Commission [CQC], 2011), nor have the negative experiences of mental health services reported by Black communities. In 2016, the Council of Europe's European Commission on Racism and Intolerance raised concerns about racism and discrimination faced by people from African and Caribbean communities in UK mental health services (European Commission Against Racism & Intolerance [ECRI], 2016).

New circles of fear?: Muslim communities and mental health services

It seems timely to ask whether we are at risk of creating new 'circles of fear' between Muslim communities and mental health services. We would argue that key ingredients for circles of fear are present. Firstly, the 'othering' of Muslim communities and seeing them as a threat is fully established within the British media and popular discourses. There has been widespread criticism of media reports, such as that produced by the Sun newspaper in November 2015, stating that a poll found that nearly one in five British Muslims support ISIS. This article was described as 'significantly misleading' by the Independent Press Standards Organisation, which found it to be in breach of the accuracy clause of the editors' code. Similarly, there has been criticism of a recent Channel 4 documentary, 'What British Muslims really think', presented by Trevor Phillips, in which British Muslims' attitudes are compared to those of the general population and are generally presented as illiberal and threatening to 'British values'. The research on which it was based has been described as both dangerous and wrong (e.g. Akeel, 2016). The government's Prevent strategy has also been accused of targeting Muslims and putting Muslim people under suspicion of 'thought crimes' (e.g. Summerfield, 2016) and eroding trust between Muslim communities and health and education systems (Open Society Foundations, 2016).

Another key ingredient for circles of fear is the widespread ignorance, stereotypes and fear among non-Muslims about Islam, including among therapists. The religiosity gap between therapists and their clients has been recognised for some time, with psychotherapy generally being seen as a secular discipline with secular beliefs and therapists are much less likely than their clients to espouse religious views (e.g. Bergin, Payne, & Richards, 1996). Harbidge (2015) conducted research with clinical psychologists working in refugee services about the extent to which they address religion and spirituality with their clients. Although she did not ask specifically about Islam, some of the views expressed by her participants included the following:

> I think the word ... 'Muslim' has different connotations now and it's linked with ideas about terrorism and religion and Islam.' (Harbidge, 2015, p. 77)

> I'm terribly aware of the sort of awful … polarizations that are happening with ISIS and the radicalization of young people … There is this kind of connect between religion and being primitive. (Harbidge, 2015, p. 76)

As these powerful and troubling quotes indicate, Islam was clearly seen by these psychologists as connected to violence, unreason and terrorism.

In our local research and consultation with Bangladeshi and Somali communities in Tower Hamlets, community members suggested that the policing of Muslim communities and the discourse of radicalization was causing distress and possibly even depression in Muslim people, especially young people, who find that important aspects of their identity are under suspicion and pathologised. Similar ideas have been expressed by writers and academics (e.g. Alam, 2016). Muir (2016) conducted qualitative research on barriers to talking therapies in Bangladeshi and Somali communities in Tower Hamlets and one of the key themes she identified was 'landscapes of mistrust', which highlighted the fears people have of speaking openly about issues such as faith and of disbelief or misunderstanding from professionals, as illustrated by these quotes:

> I think there's been a lot of trust lost within this (Bangladeshi) community in terms of mainstream services … because of what's happening in mainstream media and around the world there's a lot more cautiousness, in terms of what you say and how you say it.

> I just feel like it's getting worse because your religion is becoming one of those things that's more… people are more worried about speaking now because of what's happening all over the media and everything …

> Their houses have been raided, they have been questioned under the Terrorism Act but you say that to a therapist – would you see that as a delusion or would you see that as paranoia or would you see that as reality?

Given the existence of these ingredients for new circles of fear to develop between Muslim communities and mental health services, we believe that there is a need to build trust and to break these circles of fear, below we share some examples of how we have tried to do this in our work.

Our work with faith communities

Islam teaches us that maintaining health and seeking treatment when necessary is an individual's duty. Muslims are taught to receive illness, whether it is related to physical or mental health, with patience and prayer. Illness, like other life events, should be considered as a test from Allah (God) and not as a form of punishment but rather as a form of purification. There are treatments that Prophet Muhammad advised as being beneficial to those unwell which include praying, reciting the Qur'an, receiving counsel, or other activities that can be seen as beneficial for a person. A person who has mental illness should not be considered a stigma according to the Islamic teachings.

My team leader encouraged me to reach out to the Muslim community, especially focusing on a particular group of the community who are leaders, that is, Imams who serve the community in marriage, birth and death rites and rituals and on other various issues of the community. It was very simple for me to go into the community and communicate with the Imams as I am an Imam. We could understand each other, there was trust, our experiences connected; we were in a safe place.

Our organisations came together to hold a mental health workshop with the Imams at the local Muslim Centre, with the aim of increasing trust and understanding and to think about ways of working together. There were approximately 30 Imams representing the East London boroughs and beyond. The session was considered a great success following the rich, insightful and moving discussions that were had. The Imams shared their experiences of supporting people experiencing mental distress in the community, giving examples of how they draw on Islamic teachings and guidance to do so. As an example, one person was helping someone with financial difficulty by supporting the person with Islamic teachings and guidance. Imams shared their experience of supporting people with personal issues and family issues, such as bereavement and relationship problems. All this was done in a safe place where they were able to express their faith and values with comfort and ease. There was also a real sense of enthusiasm and a wish for further understanding as well as continued collaboration between the faith leaders and mental health professionals.

Further training sessions were requested and the next collaboration was on 'Substance misuse' which was also a huge success. It had a mixed variety of people including female participants from the community who came from a variety of backgrounds such as Imams, students, health advocates, youth and charity workers. Further actions include a request for ongoing dialogue between Imams, scholars, mental health professionals and traditional faith healers to find common ground and improve the links between the different places in the community where people seek help.

Faith in recovery: making talking therapies relevant to Muslim communities

An important aspect of reducing the effects of 'circles of fear' is to make talking therapies more accessible for minority communities. Our model involves working in partnership with BME voluntary sector groups and tailoring interventions to the needs and strengths of communities. The Tree of Life/ Faith in Recovery approach (Mustafa & Byrne, 2016) was developed in response to feedback from communities indicating that, if psychological therapy was seen as more holistic, for example, incorporating people's faith and religion, it would be more acceptable and relevant to community members. We developed an intervention in partnership with a local mental health charity, who helped design and deliver sessions that would be relevant to their Bangladeshi and Somali service users. The sessions were delivered in Bengali/Sylheti and in Somali by workers from the charity and our team. The contributions from our Imam were highly valued by the participants.

The intervention used the Tree of Life (Ncube, 2006) narrative therapy approach which views the client as the expert and supports participants to develop their own preferred stories from a position of strength, hope and recovery. This approach is increasingly used in mental health services, in both in-patient and community settings and has proved effective at improving accessibility and acceptability of psychological therapy for African and Caribbean men (Byrne et al., 2011; Carlin, 2009; Griffiths et al., 2012).

It was clear in both the Bangladeshi and Somali groups that faith and spirituality played a central role in most participants' lives as evident from the drawing of their trees. For example, Islam was frequently represented as a strength of the participants, pilgrimage to hajj as one of their hopes for the future and the Qur'an as a gift that has been given to them. Within a focus group evaluation participants also stated, for example, 'I'm a Muslim and that's the core' and 'I leave a lot to Allah because we trust him'.

Sessions were co-produced with the participants to reflect the importance they placed on Islamic ideas of wellbeing and dealing with trials and tribulations in their lives. Participants reported the most important aspect of the Faith in Recovery approach was the way they were supported to explore the meaning of difficulties as spoken about in the Qur'an. The Imam in our team facilitated discussion on two surahs (chapters) which speak of trials by using the Prophet Muhammad's life experiences. Surah Adh Dhuna (The Morning Hours) and Surah Ash Shahr (The Relief).

In the extract below, one participant of the Bangladeshi men's group shares his experience. This extract was previously published in Context magazine (Mustafa & Byrne, 2016).

> I've been attending Mind for the last four years and I only attend Bangladeshi men's group. This is because I feel comfortable and share experiences. When I heard that a guest speaker will join us and we will be doing a course my first thought was 'No not again'. I was guessing that it was them 'money advice sessions' but when I heard the words Tree of Life I thought to myself 'hold on, this could be interesting'. Then we were told a psychologist is running the group with us, which interested me the most. This is because I've been with the forensic services for the last five years and I learnt so much from psychologists that I have a huge respect for them. Since they was the one that made me look into my life and where I went wrong and what issues I had. I see psychologists like mirrors they help you reflect your personality so that you may be aware of the issues you may have. When we started the Tree of Life I was keen to learn and take whatever I can from the group which one day will be helpful to me. It was interesting to find out a lot of us had similarities as well as differences on how we see the world and what is important to us. We found that religion is important to all of us. As we progressed in the group, we spoke about religion. We explored

> and found out that there were so many similarities between religion and psychology. I was amazed about the fact psychology is tapping into religion in some way so I asked a question, 'Who came up with this idea?' so they said they are doing a trial. I thought 'Wow!'. I sometimes feel lonely. I live on my own. Some days I feel that I have no future. Until I heard about a verse of the Qur'an which talks about the time when the prophet didn't get any contact from God for six months he thought God was upset with him. But God said 'Don't be sad. I haven't forgotten about you, neither am I upset with you', which gave me hope that just because nothing positive is happening in your life doesn't mean God doesn't love you or has forgotten about you. I've learnt this part of the Qur'an is a remedy for depression, which was interesting. What I've gained, I wish other people gain what I've gained from the group.

Qualitative evaluation highlighted the importance of the group and shared understandings; faith as central to wellbeing and recovery; hope and the importance of a safe space to express what's important to participants. Participants repeatedly spoke of their surprise that we were exploring these Islamic ideas with them. Although they spoke openly about how faith supports them in their own lives, there was a real feeling that this is kept separate to discussions with mental health professionals especially with those who do not come from the same religious background. Participants were aware of the potential risks of talking about their religion and requested support around how to bring up ideas of faith in sessions with mental health professionals and for mental health professionals to be trained to better understand Islam and the centrality of faith in recovery.

It is of real concern to us that Muslim service users do not feel comfortable talking about what is important to them in their recovery within mainstream mental health services as this feeds into the' circles of fear' and 'landscapes of mistrust' identified earlier. The difficulty of speaking about religion in general and Islam in particular is also something we have experienced as professionals. We have noticed that, whenever we speak about our work together, we are met with certain reactions and questions that have made us reflect on how the 'circles of fear' or 'landscapes of mistrust' can also affect our relationships with colleagues. For example, regardless of the actual topic we are presenting, we are often called on to explain or defend Islam, to account for its perceived teachings on women's rights, homosexuality or apostasy. Our motivations for doing the work have been questioned, despite what we feel to be a robust rationale. Features of our work, which are entirely familiar within mental health settings, such as the provision of a single-sex group, has been seen as troubling. We can only conclude that it is because of the perceived connection to religion and imagined values underlying this.

Conclusion

The discourse of radicalisation and resulting 'circles of fear' present huge challenges and risks to the relationships between Muslim communities and mental health services. They prevent people speaking openly about their fears and the importance of their faith and may ultimately prevent people from accessing mainstream mental health services, especially if these services are perceived as suspicious of people's religion and ignorant of the social and political contexts in which they are living. Despite the challenges highlighted, we believe it is possible to develop a positive spiral driven by trust and collaboration. Our experience has taught us that we can begin to break the 'circles of fear' by working in partnership with community groups and faith leaders; building trust based on mutual respect and appreciation of each other's expertise; understanding and valuing Islam as a core aspect of people's identity and a preferred way of coping and bringing the learning back into the statutory services, creating space for dialogue. Our hope is that, as services become more confident to explore faith, culture and discrimination, service users will be more willing to engage and that ultimately, we can provide services in a more responsive way. However, we must be aware that the focus on radicalisation carries the risk of entrenching 'circles of fear' and alienating the communities we hope to reach.

Acknowledgements

We would like to thank Nigel Copsy, Team Leader of the Department of Spiritual, Religious and Cultural Care and Patricia Potter, Head of Tower Hamlets Psychology, East London Foundation Trust for their ongoing support. We also wish to thank the London Muslim Centre, East London Mosque and Mind in Tower Hamlets and Newham for collaborating with us in this work.

Disclosure statement

No potential conflict of interest was reported by the authors.

References

Akeel, M. (2016, April 12). Trevor Phillips' research on British Muslims is dangerous and wrong. No wonder Islamophobia is on the rise. *Independent Newspaper*.

Alam, A. (2016, February). The mental trauma caused by Prevent on Muslim children. *5Pillars*.

Bergin, A. E., Payne, I. R., & Richards, P. S. (1996). Values in psychotherapy. In E. P. Shafranske (Ed.), *Religion and the clinical practice of psychology* (pp. 297–325). Washington, DC: American Psychological Association.

Byrne, A., Warren, A., Joof, B., Johnson, D., Casimir, L., Hinds, C., … Griffiths, S. (2011). 'A powerful piece of work': African and Caribbean men talking about the tree of life. *Context, 117*, 40–45.

Care Quality Commission. (2011). *Count Me In Census, 2010*. London: Author.

Carlin, M. (2009). *Trailblazers: An introduction to talking therapies for African and Caribbean men with mental health problems: An evaluation report*. London: Mellow; East London NHS Foundation Trust.

European Commission Against Racism and Intolerance. (2016). *ECRI report on the United Kingdom*. Strasbourg: Council of Europe.

Griffiths, S., Byrne, A., & Nolas, S. (2010). *Trailblazers: Improving access to talking therapies for African and Caribbean men Phase II: An evaluation report*. London: Mellow; East London NHS Foundation Trust.

Harbidge, P. R. (2015). *An exploration of how clinical psychologists make sense of the roles of religious and spiritual beliefs within their therapeutic work with adults who have experienced trauma* (Unpublished thesis). University of East London.

Keating, F., Robertson, D., McCulloch, A., & Frances, E. (2002). *Breaking the circles of fear: A review of the relationship between mental health services and African and Caribbean communities*. London: Sainsbury Centre for Mental Health.

Keating, F., & Robertson, D. (2004). Fear, black people and mental illness: A vicious circle? *Health and Social Care in the Community, 12*, 439–447.

Muir, J. (2016). *An exploration of the barriers to talking therapies that Bangladeshi communities in an inner-city London borough encounter* (Unpublished service-related research report). University of East London.

Mustafa, S., & Byrne, A. (2016). Faith in recovery: Adapting the tree of life to include Islamic ideas of wellbeing. *Context, 146*, 10–14.

Ncube, N. (2006). The tree of life project: Using narrative ideas in work with vulnerable children in Southern Africa. *The International Journal of Narrative Therapy and Community Work, 1*, 3–16.

Open Society Foundations. (2016). *Eroding Trust: The UK's prevent counter-extremism strategy in health and education*. New York, NY: Author.

Prins, H., Backer-Holst, T., Francis, E., & Keitch, I. (1993). *Report of the Committee of Inquiry into the death in Broadmoor Hospital of Orville Blackwood and a review of the deaths of two other Afro-Caribbean patients. Big, Black and Dangerous?* The Special Hospitals Service Authority.

Summerfield, D. (2016). Mandating doctors to attend counter-terrorism workshops is medically unethical. *British Journal of Psychiatry Bulletin, 40*, 87–88.

The challenge of radicalisation: a public health approach to understanding and intervention

Kamaldeep Bhui and Edgar Jones

Radicalisation is the term proposed to explain how an apparently ordinary person can be transformed from a law-abiding citizen into a supporter of violent protest. It refers to a process of belief modification and requires a progression from feeling sympathy towards violence for a political goal to direct involvement in such activities. This paper explores the reasons why individuals are drawn to extreme movements and how approaches devised for public health can be applied to prevention. We argue for interventions at an early stage when ideas are beginning to take root in people vulnerable to the recruiter's message and identify both protective and risk factors.

Introduction

Since 9/11 the focus on terrorism and its prevention is central to government initiatives around the world, whether high- or low-income countries, or whether dominated by radical religious belief systems or practices, or secular right-wing movements (Felton, 2004; Frank, 2005). Terrorism undermines societies and institutions by killing civilians and diverting resources, especially in low-income countries, from other important humanitarian, health and societally critical policies and programmes (Bhui, Hicks, Lashley, & Jones, 2012; Goldman, 2002). Whilst governments have introduced measures designed to address radicalisation (in the UK the Contest model includes a Prevent programme, whilst Channel is designed to counter beliefs and actions likely to lead to violent protest), there remains less emphasis on understanding the roots of disaffection and grievances with democratic processes (HM Government, 2011). This paper explores a range of ideas proposed to explain the power of radical philosophies and why they are so appealing to groups of young people to the extent that many are willing to sacrifice their lives.

An evolving context

War and conflict have focused attention on psychological trauma. The reified concept of post-traumatic stress has helped to justify access to health care for asylum seekers and refugees, civilians exposed to war but trapped in the conflict zones, veterans returning from combat, and those that are victims of physical assault, crime, rape, or violent attack, or natural disasters (Jacobs, Burns, & Gross, 2003). Terrorism is now added to this list of trauma, both for its direct effects on those at the heart of a bomb attack or killing, and for its indirect effects through the fear invoked in family and friends of victims, ordinary citizens and witnesses, including children and young people for whom terrorism is daily mentioned on the news channels (Rousseau & Measham, 2004). Yet terrorism is not only an individual experience but also a group one, designed to undermine a particular set of core values about society and replace them with 'higher' causes that do not always seek rational earthly solutions, or goals that political compromise might deliver (Atran, 2003, 2010). Such attacks have a symbolic effect and are designed to destroy core values of democracy. Many of the recent attacks are directed towards events and activities where people express freedoms: a gay nightclub in Orlando, a Jewish supermarket in Paris, or the Copenhagen shootings at a public afternoon event called 'Art, Blasphemy and Freedom of Expression' and the killing of a Jewish security guard outside the city's Great Synagogue in February 2015 (Anderson, 2016). Although individual people are targets, the goal of most terrorists is politically or culturally recognisable groups, including governments (Alderdice, 2009; Gostin, 2002).

Yet, what do we know about the causes of terrorism in order to prevent it? Generally, it is thought that there are socially strained contexts in which terrorism emerges as a possible option for those feeling disempowered (Leiken, 2016), but this still does not fully explain the chosen methods and their extreme and violent nature. The chosen method may reflect a politically isolated minority (usually) to wage (an unequal) war with those in power, in order to change the political decisions of those in power and to disrupt ordinary processes of government and governance. Instilling fear in citizens is part of that process (Leistedt, 2016; McGilloway, Ghosh, & Bhui, 2015). This inequality in power, that is an ostensibly weaker authority attacking a larger more powerful one, is given prominence in the narratives of terrorists in order to justify the atrocities, killings and the persistent disruption to society (O'Shaughnessy & Baines, 2009). Yet at the same time, recent claims from IS (Islamic State) and al-Qaeda is that they are larger authorities themselves, seeking to subvert a whole political and religious system and to exchange it for their own, and the active and rapid pace of communications, the levels of resources, and use of persuasive device (technological, digital and dramatic) are alarming and distinct from previous terrorist groups (Bhui & Ibrahim, 2013; Neumann, 2016).

Justifications for such acts include religious ideology, even if this falls well beyond an orthodox interpretation of faith, political discrimination and powerlessness such that the subjects' only option for action includes violence (Atran, 2003, 2010; Baines et al., 2010). However, many people feel aggrieved but choose democratic and non-violent political protest; and even where protest becomes violent, for example, riots in North London by black youth, the state of anarchy is quickly resolved and order restored whilst lessons are learnt. Yet, terrorism persists and the so-called 'fifth wave' under the auspices of Islamic authorities, such as al-Qaeda and the Islamic State, have assumed a brutal and repressive character, using technologically advanced communications and persuasive technologies to recruit and persuade. These narratives seek to frame terrorist actions in a context of righteousness and the protection of the broader Muslim faith, appealing to individuals, often young and impressionable, looking for a purpose and meaning in their lives, a political search for belonging rather than a social or health malady (McGarry, 2016).

Mental illness and terrorism

Mental illness is a global problem, even in high income countries, and yet only between a quarter and a third of those with a common psychological disorder receive any form of treatment; the absence of treatment is lower for those with psychosis, but in lower income countries the indices are far worse, with very little spent on mental health of citizens. Terrorism is known to inflict experiences of loss and trauma, and so is often, like conflict and war in general, associated with depression, anxiety, post-traumatic stress or abnormal grief. However, mental health experts have recently turned their attention to prevention of terrorism by trying to understand the motivations and sentiments of those recruited to undertake violent acts against innocent civilians. Historically, terrorism has been broadly recognised as a political act with little relationship to mental illness other than causing mass group and individual distress. However, the recent phenomenon of citizens of Western democracies taking up terrorist causes in the countries in which they were educated, or seeking out terrorist networks in Syria or Iraq or Afghanistan, has raised questions about who is susceptible to recruitment narratives. So understanding psychological processes by which individuals align with extremist thinking and are motivated to act violently is a key issue for modern democracies. Another growing concern is that some people who already appear to suffer emotional distress or frank mental illness may be particularly at risk from terrorist propaganda. More specifically, lone actors, those not belonging to any terror networks in a command and control manner, but people who are nonetheless appearing to act on behalf of a terrorist cause, are thought to be more likely to suffer from mental illness (Corner & Gill, 2015).

Our work has sought to understand prevention through the very early phases of radicalisation, following the analysis of New York 9/11 perpetrators (Silber & Bhatt, 2007). That is, how might we stop people early in the trajectory of becoming involved in violent acts of terrorism, long before they have even considered violence as an action? This is not popular work nor always well received. As some believed that this approach inadvertently mitigated the gravity of terrorism offences by explaining them in terms of understandable psychological processes and mental illness. Others felt that we risked stigmatising those with psychological disorders, already perceived in the public imagination to be dangerous, such that people with mental illnesses would worry about receiving treatment and those around them would fear them more. Then, other objections to such work are that terrorism is fundamentally a political issue relating to security and should be addressed through domestic and international policy through counterterrorism agencies.

The existing government strategy, strong and successful as it is on preventing incidents by high-risk individuals linked to specific groups, does not consider prevention at the earliest phases. The Royal College of Psychiatrists issued a position statement in September 2016 emphasising that the evidence upon which public bodies are asked to change practice to protect individuals at risk of being drawn into terrorism is limited (https://www.rcpsych.ac.uk/pdf/PS04_16.pdf). The statement also observed that safeguarding is already taking place in the context of good psychiatric practice, and that managing risk is part and parcel of mental health care. Furthermore, in the context of terrorism risk prediction tools are doomed to fail, given the rarity of the event. In anticipation of this evidential context from 2008 onwards, Bhui, Jones and others began to explore public health approaches to radicalisation, the process proposed to explain the engagement of ordinary young people in terrorist causes. Does radicalisation exist? Is it measurable? Our research efforts aimed to explore this, but in close collaboration with communities who were already complaining that government strategy excluded them and perhaps even diminished their role as suspect communities.

Public health

Whilst acts of terrorism remain mercifully rare, they are dwarfed by public health problems such as TB, infectious diseases, accidents and death from road accidents or due to cancer, obesity or heart disease. Although there has been a dramatic increase in the last six months in the numbers of people killed by terrorist attacks in the UK, which have rightly caused widespread alarm and concern, since 7/7 there have only been, at the time of writing (June 2017), 39 deaths as a result of terrorism within the UK: Mohammed Saleem, a 82-year old Muslim stabbed by Pavlo Lapshyn, a 25-year old Ukrainian student in April 2013, Private Lee Rigby stabbed in May 2013 by Michael Adebolajo and Michael Adebowale near the Royal Artillery Barracks in Woolwich, Jo Cox killed by Thomas Mair in June 2016, the five who died on Westminster Bridge in March 2017, 22 killed by a suicide bomber in Manchester, eight killed in the London Bridge in attack, and one person in an attack at a mosque in Finsbury Park in June 2017. The rarity of terrorist acts makes it very difficult for any science of risk prediction or prevention to be certain about preventive capability. However, we also know that terrorists are technologically advanced and adaptive, so that whatever preventive efforts are introduced, they are rapidly superseded by events.

Despite the rarity, terrorism continues to attract much government attention and finance, because it symbolically attacks the heart of a society's cultural values, governance processes and structures of law and order, 'so that people can go about their lives freely with confidence' (HM Government, 2011)

A public health approach

Public health approaches involve close connections with the community, actions at a population level and not only through health agencies, and interventions that aims to reduce risk factors and promote protective factors. The purpose is to shift the distribution of risk factors in a population to reduce the number of people who are reaching the threshold for having significant risks and developing illness. This approach has been applied to violence prevention in general (Mikton, Butchart, Dahlberg, & Krug, 2016), and to behaviours such as suicide, violence, drug taking, crime and now also to radicalisation and terrorism (Bhui et al., 2012).

A good exemplar is public health approaches to violence and conflict seek to enact prevention at the earliest opportunity (Sidel & Levy, 2003). These approaches have been applied to violence prevention in general, to teenage pregnancy, gun and violent crime, as well as smoking and other societal ills that, if unaddressed, consume significant health care resources (Henry, Farrell, & The Multisite Violence Prevention Project, 2004; Massetti, Holland, & Gorman-Smith, 2016; Mikhail & Nemeth, 2016; Mikton et al., 2016). Suicide, for example, is a rare event but identifying risk factors associated with suicide in the general population such as self-harming behaviours, alcohol and drug misuse, depression, access to means (firearms, coal gas) will plausibly reduce rates. The purpose of a population-level intervention is to shift the risk factor profile of any early indicator towards the left so reducing the likelihood of adverse outcomes. However, to reduce the incidence of radicalisation and violent protest, we need to better understand the social and psychological conditions that lie on the pathway. Therein lies the dilemma; we do not know enough about the pathways and these are likely to be multi-layered and multi-faceted, appealing to different groups of vulnerable or susceptible individuals.

To investigate what radicalisation might look like, as part of a large research programme, we worked with local communities to better understand the meaning of radicalisation and how to measure it. This culminated in a survey of over 600 Pakistani and Bangladeshi men and women living in the community. The methodology, and detailed analyses are already published and accessible (Bhui, Everitt, & Jones, 2014; Ghosh et al., 2013). Although extremism is not limited to South Asian or Muslim heritage populations, these were the groups that were under scrutiny and to whom many of the debates about radicalisation related. Thus, we collected views from community groups to construct a set of questions which were later piloted, tested, and refined and included in a survey of Bangladeshi and Pakistani men and women. We discovered that people were willing to answer the questions, that there were no incidents during our survey and that such work was possible. The research enabled us to develop a measure of sympathies for radicalisation, and consider the relevance of a number of variables that showed correlations with our measure.

- Relevant
    - Relative social isolation
    - Moderate to high social capital
    - Youth
    - Non-migrant status, that is born in UK
- Not relevant
    - Poverty
    - Discrimination
    - Total life events
    - Depressive symptoms measured on a continuous scale using PHQ-9
    - Anxiety measured on GAD-7
    - Religiosity

These findings challenged the prevailing view that feeling oppressed, marginalised or being of low income were essential drivers of grievances, that then led to anger and thus potential recruitment into radicalised thinking. Of course, although we attempted to recruit a population sample, our study is limited to inferences about our specific samples. It is possible that of those who progress towards more active involvement, there are additional factors, that we have not been able to consider. Taking a public health perspective also meant that we should also consider those who were not so condemning of terrorist acts, and thus might be open to persuasion, that is to view the spectrum of sympathy to condemnation as a continuum rather than being concerned with only those actively professing sympathies for violent causes including terrorism. In this manner, we found depressive symptoms, and scores above 5 on the PHQ-9 were relevant and related to greater sympathy rather than condemnation of such acts. This lead us to investigate what depressive symptoms might mean and their role (Bhui, Warfa, & Jones, 2014; Bhui et al., 2014). To what extent was this hopelessness or pessimism, leading to a search for meaning and purpose, or was depression related to personality and not something that might come to the attention of psychotherapists. We are undertaking further research on what types of depressive symptoms are relevant, and comparing White British with Pakistani men and women to explore common factors relating to extremism. A recent analysis of this data shows that depressive symptoms increase sympathies for violent protest and terrorist a little, but surprisingly life events, especially bereavement and giving money to a charity, and to a less significant extent, political participation, are negatively correlated with sympathies; our interpretation is that social connectedness, even if expressed through loss, is protective (Bhui, Silva, Topciu, & Jones, 2016).

Thus relationships and the ability to tackle pessimistic thinking seem important, but so does being part of a community and giving to that community. Focusing only on attitudes or psychological constructs as targets of deradicalisation might seem an obvious way forward, given the parallels with psychological therapies that target cognitive biases. However, there are wider social drivers and more internal and collective sacred antecedents that would not easily be accessible. Deradicalisation programmes around the world do make use of the social and cultural milieu of the individual and their identity group within which psychological or other work can be undertaken. For example, see the reports from the Radicalisation Awareness Network (https://www.counterextremism.org/resources/details/id/310/ran-deradicalisation-working-group-proposed-policy-recommendations). Indeed, this is also the way offender management services operate. However, a population approach takes a different perspective, that of intervening early in the natural history of developing extreme ideologies, and focusing on prevention at a population level, exposing all people to the right sorts of messages and counter-narratives, and to tackle the social drivers and potential sources of grievance and isolation that may encourage people to seek empowering and powerful but dangerous ideologies to give their lives meaning.

Clearly, the public health approach is there to complement and not to replace criminal justice agencies, especially if people have moved more towards joining and participating in organised groups or personal individual actions in support of terrorist organisations. The public approach also seeks to reduce fear and provide practical and evidence based information to the wider public, so that all can see themselves as part of a solution, rather than be excluded or even feel they are the suspect community. Part of the strategy of terrorism is to provoke a harsh counter-response that reinforces accusations of discrimination and alienation and injustice against groups, most prominently against Muslim populations and countries in the Middle East. However, thoughtful and measured responses are necessary, not dissimilar to what was seen during the Norwegian legal process after the Brevik incident. When atrocities and homicide are seen in unusual and often idiosyncratic circumstances from people not expected to commit those acts, the public and police seek explanation, and invoking mental illness or psychological processes are now common. This may further stigmatise people with mental illness and those seeking help from psychological services. We do need to promote an evidence base, but for now we know the majority of incidents have little to do with mental illness, and the extent of modifiable psychological process or vulnerability is yet to be determined. This field of research and practice is in its infancy and can learn much from existing literature on crime and violence, and experiences of recognising and preventing crime in general. However, the dimensions of culture, religiosity, international politics and world crises and conflict, do bring a different dimension. The place of psychoanalytic thought lies in not only interrogating the evidence and emotional processes of perpetrators, but also of political decision makers and victims, and the wider public.

Conclusion

An analysis of media responses to our nuanced population studies showed that the press often occupy polarised positions, suggesting that the capacity for emotional distortion is high in relation to violence and terrorism. The studies were based on proportional quota sampling of people of Muslim heritage in defined areas and yet the findings were interpreted by newspapers as if we had interviewed convicted terrorists. Furthermore, there was concern that we were dismissing terrorism as a form of mental illness, or that we had ignored accumulated understanding of different varieties of terrorism in Northern Ireland and other countries. Strategies to reduce the impact of radical messages should be based on a gradual but evolving process of gathering information and knowledge and to resist the temptation to reach for a binary position on findings and policy implications. Binary thinking is a core challenge we face when tackling terrorism, a rejection of possibilities that are not in accord with our own precepts. This tendency is seen not only in researchers, practitioners and experts, but also amongst government leads and politicians. The notion of preventive efforts introduced long before any chance of a commitment to violence seemed irrelevant to some at the front line of counterterrorism for whom the imminent threat is the priority. Whilst their legitimate and pressing concern for public safety is acknowledged, greater regard should be given to addressing what seems like an endless supply of people willing to give their lives to terrorist causes. Drawing on writings of Atran (2003, 2010), loyalty to intimate cohorts of peers, often promoted through religious communion, seem relevant, whilst a search for meaning and purpose may draw many away from a secure life with their families towards radical extremism.

Disclosure statement

No potential conflict of interest was reported by the authors.

References

Alderdice, J. T. (2009). Sacred values: Psychological and anthropological perspectives on fairness, fundamentalism, and terrorism. *Annals of the New York Academy of Sciences, 1167*, 158–173. doi:10.1111/j.1749-6632.2009.04510.x

Anderson, D. (2016, April, 26). *Terrorism and the law*. Graham Turnbull Lecture, Law Society, 5–6. Retrieved from https://www.google.co.uk/#q=Anderson,+D.+(2016,+April,+26).+Terrorism+and+the+law.+Graham+Turnbull+Lecture+Law&spf=1500468358349

Atran, S. (2003). Genesis of suicide terrorism. *Science, 299*, 1534–1539. doi:10.1126/science.1078854

Atran, S. (2010). *Taking to the enemy, violent extremism, sacred values, and what it means to be human*. London: Allen Lane.

Baines, P. R., O'Shaughnessy, N. J., Moloney, K., Richards, B., Butler, S., & Gill, M. (2010). The dark side of political marketing: Islamist propaganda, reversal theory and British Muslims. *European Journal of Marketing, 44*, 478–495. doi:10.1108/03090561011020543

Bhui, K., Everitt, B., & Jones, E. (2014). Might depression, psychosocial adversity, and limited social assets explain vulnerability to and resistance against violent radicalisation? *PLoS ONE, 9*, e105918. doi:10.1371/journal.pone.0105918

Bhui, K., & Ibrahim, Y. (2013). Marketing the 'radical': Symbolic communication and persuasive technologies in jihadist websites. *Transcultural Psychiatry, 50*, 216–234. doi:10.1177/1363461513479329

Bhui, K., Silva, M. J., Topciu, R. A., & Jones, E. (2016). Pathways to sympathies for violent protest and terrorism. *The British Journal of Psychiatry, 209*, 483–490. doi:10.1192/bjp.bp.116.185173

Bhui, K., Warfa, N., & Jones, E. (2014). Is violent radicalisation associated with poverty, migration, poor self-reported health and common mental disorders? *PLoS ONE, 9*, e90718. doi:10.1371/journal.pone.0090718

Bhui, K. S., Hicks, M. H., Lashley, M., & Jones, E. (2012). A public health approach to understanding and preventing violent radicalization. *BMC Medicine, 10*, 186. doi:10.1186/1741-7015-10-16

Corner, E., & Gill, P. (2015). A false dichotomy? Mental illness and lone-actor terrorism. *Law and Human Behavior, 39*, 23–34. doi:10.1037/lhb0000102

Felton, C. J. (2004). Lessons learned since September 11th 2001 concerning the mental health impact of terrorism, appropriate response strategies and future preparedness. *Psychiatry: Interpersonal and Biological Processes, 67*, 147–152. doi:10.1521/psyc.67.2.147.35957

Frank, E. (2005). Funding the public health response to terrorism. *BMJ, 331*, E378–E379. doi:10.1136/bmj.331.7517.E378

Ghosh, P., Warfa, N., McGilloway, A., Ali, I., Jones, E., & Bhui, K. (2013). Violent radicalisation and recruitment to terrorism: Perspectives of wellbeing and social cohesion of citizens of muslim heritage. *Sociology Mind, 3*, 7. doi:10.4236/sm.2013.34039

Goldman, W. (2002). Best practices: Terrorism and mental health: Private-sector responses and issues for policy makers. *Psychiatric Services, 53*, 941–943. doi:10.1176/appi.ps.53.8.941

Gostin, L. O. (2002). Public health law in an age of terrorism: Rethinking individual rights and common goods. *Health Affairs, 21*, 79–93.

Henry, D. B., & Farrell, A. D., The Multisite Violence Prevention Project (2004). The study designed by a committee: Design of the Multisite Violence Prevention Project. *American Journal of Preventive Medicine, 26*, 12–19.

HM Government. (2011). *Contest: The UK Government's strategy for countering terrorism*. London. Retrieved from https://www.gov.uk/government/publications/counter-terrorism-strategy-contest

Jacobs, L. M., Burns, K. J., & Gross, R. I. (2003). Terrorism: A public health threat with a trauma system response. *Journal of Trauma and Acute Care Surgery, 55*, 1014–1021. doi:10.1097/01.TA.0000084515.74480.BA

Leiken, R. (2016). *Europe's angry Muslims, the revolt of the second generation*. Oxford: Oxford University Press.

Leistedt, S. J. (2016). On the radicalization process. *Journal of Forensic Sciences, 61*, 1588–1591. doi:10.1111/1556-4029.13170

Massetti, G. M., Holland, K. M., & Gorman-Smith, D. (2016). Implementation measurement for evidence-based violence prevention programs in communities. *Journal of Community Health, 41*, 881–894. doi:10.1007/s10900-016-0156-z

McGarry, P. J. (2016). Terrorism: It's not mental illness – it's politics. *BJPsych Bulletin, 40*, 285. doi:10.1192/pb.40.5.285a

McGilloway, A., Ghosh, P., & Bhui, K. (2015). A systematic review of pathways to and processes associated with radicalization and extremism amongst Muslims in Western societies. *International Review of Psychiatry, 27*, 39–50. doi:10.3109/09540261.2014.992008

Mikhail, J. N., & Nemeth, L. S. (2016). Trauma center based youth violence prevention programs: An integrative review. *Trauma Violence Abuse, 17*, 500–519. doi:10.1177/1524838015584373

Mikton, C. R., Butchart, A., Dahlberg, L. L., & Krug, E. G. (2016). Global status report on violence prevention 2014. *American Journal of Preventive Medicine, 50*, 652–659. doi:10.1016/j.amepre.2015.10.007

Neumann, P. (2016). *Radicalised: New jihadists and the threat to the West*. London: I.B.Tauris.

O'Shaughnessy, N. J., & Baines, P. R. (2009). Selling terror: The symbolization and positioning of Jihad. *Marketing Theory, 9*, 227–241. doi:10.1177/1470593109103069

Rousseau, C., & Measham, T. (2004). Childhood reactions to terrorism. *Journal of the American Academy of Child & Adolescent Psychiatry, 43*, 1320–1321. doi:10.1097/01.chi.0000138357.36723.6e

Sidel, V. W., & Levy, B. S. (2003). War, terrorism, and public health. *The Journal of Law, Medicine & Ethics, 31*, 516–523.

Silber, M., & Bhatt, A. (2007). *Radicalization in the West: The homegrown threat*. New York, NY: OccupyBawStreet.com Press.

Index

addictive violence 62
Adebolajo, Michael 2, 131
Adebowale, Michael 2, 131
Adh Dhuna (The Morning Hours) 124
adolescence 3, 70–2, 76–80, 100, 115
affective aggression 62
Afghanistan 6, 16, 21, 41, 56, 84, 99, 100, 130
African National Congress (ANC) 57, 58
aggregation and massification 10–11
aggression 3, 15, 56–7, 90; affective 62; fear and 44; predatory 62; and violence 8, 63–6, 96
Ahmad, K. 41, 42
Akhtar, S. 9, 13, 97
Alderdice, J. L. 1–3, 53–6, 111, 112
Alderdice, J. T. 98, 101
Alderdice, L. 7
al-Qaeda 2, 19, 32, 109, 110, 129, 130
Alvarez, Anne 3
ANC *see* African National Congress (ANC)
ancient regime 52–3
anger 19, 25, 29, 33, 43, 62, 63, 86, 106, 133
Anglo-Saxon culture of Britain 23–4
The Anti-Group (Nitsun) 9–10
antisocial tendency 15
Anti-Terrorism Crime and Security Act 2001 108
Arendt, H. 95
armalite and ballot paper strategy 26
Arundale, J. 8
Ash Shahr (The Relief) 124
Atran, S. 24–5, 31, 135
Autistic Spectrum Disorder (ASD) 83

'banality of evil' 95
Bangladeshi community 5, 122, 124, 132
Bartlett, J. 96
Baumeister, R. 102
Beier, M. 73
Belfast Agreement 26
benzodiazepines 26
Bergman, A. 88
Bhui, K. 2, 5, 131
Bin Laden, Osama 7, 15, 16, 28, 51, 54
Birdwell, J. 96
bitter hatred 62–3
Black communities 121
Blackwell, D. 7
Bohleber, W. 72
Bola, J. J. 59–60
Bollas, C. 15
bombing: London suicide 94; Oklahoma 88; strategy of 26; suicide 4, 54, 84; World Trade Center 75; *see also* suicide bomber
boundaries 39–41
Bowlby, J. 90–1
Bowling for Columbine 86
'a breeding ground for violence' 101
Breivik, A. 102, 108
Brexit 33, 52, 53
Broucek, F. J. 67
Brussels airport and metro bombing 101
Buruma, I. 102
Bush administration 6, 29

caregiver, aggression 64–5
Carrapico, H. 101
Catholic Ireland 24
'Ceasefire Soldiers' 101
Channel programme 114
Charlie Hebdo shooting 2
Chechen separatists 110
children violence: deficit and neglect 66–8; disturbance and deviance 62–3; disturbance/disorder 63–5; violence and aggression 65–6

chilling fear 62
Chomsky, Noam 56
Christianity, fundamentalism 72–3
'circles of fear' 120; faith community 122–3; muslim communities and mental health services 121–2; recovery approach 123–5
civil rights 25, 29
claustro-agoraphobic dilemma 90
Clinton, Bill 107
Cold War 32, 40, 43
Collins, Michael 25
Columbine Massacre 82–3; background 85–6; clinical example 91; disclosures 89; narcissistic personality and alter-egos 88–9; narratives 86–8; psychopathology and attachment difficulties 89–91; stalking and harassment 84–5
'Columbine Myth' 86–8
communal divisions 26
communication violence 111
confidentiality and disclosure 115
contingency 67, 68
Cooper, H. H. A. 106
'core complex' 90
Corner, E. 95, 106, 107, 109–11
Counter-Terrorism and Security Act 2015 114
counter-terrorism, psychiatrist 114–15; confidentiality and disclosure 115; risk assessment tools 116; stigma 116
'Country Life' 50
Cox, Murray 48
Crenshaw, M. 95
criminality 4, 14, 15, 72, 99, 101, 103
criminal justice system 45
criminal, terrorist 101
cross-border trade 45
Csef, H. 72, 77
culture 12, 23, 24, 39, 40, 43, 46, 49, 52, 59, 86, 99, 100, 101, 106, 120, 126, 134

Daesh 6–7, 16
Dalal, F. 12–14
Davids, M. F. 12, 14
deficit and neglect (violence) 66–8
demilitarization 45
deradicalisation programme 109, 134
destruction antisocial tendency 15
De Zulueta, F. 7, 8, 11, 13, 14, 97
'disease of reality' 38
disrespect 29–31
dissolution 37–9
disturbance and deviance 62–3
disturbance/disorder (violence) 63–5
Duran, Francisco Martin 107

East/West boundary 40
economic expansionism 56
emotion 1, 5, 9, 10, 14, 23, 27–31, 36–8, 41–4, 46, 53–5, 67, 75, 85–91, 96, 103, 106, 110, 112, 113, 130, 134, 135
Emwazi, Mohammed 102
Erikson, Erik 41, 77
Europe 6, 13, 19, 24, 27, 32, 33, 44–5, 74, 77, 112
European integration 27
evolution and dissolution 37–8
Extremism Risk Guidelines (ERG 22+) 116
Ey, Henri 37–8

Fairbairn, W. R. D. 8
faith community 122–3
Faith in Recovery approach *see* The Tree of Life/Faith in Recovery approach
fear of annihilation (Hopper) 10, 14
Federal Bureau of Investigation (FBI) 112
'fifth wave' 130
Finsbury Park attack 2, 131
Fonagys proposition 8, 14
Foulkes, S. 9
Freud, S. 8, 12, 13, 36, 37, 46, 76, 77, 86, 88, 97, 111
Frosh, S. 11–12
fundamentalism 44; encapsulated 40–1; Islamic 57, 58, 77; mechanism 39; phenomenon of 41; regression into 33; religious 44, 49–52, 57, 75–9; and terrorism 1–3, 11, 14, 43, 55, 70–4
'Fundamentalism as patriarchal protest movement' (Riesebrodt) 76–7
fundamentalists and violent jihadists 42

General Medical Council (GMC) 115
Georgio 63
ghettos 55
Gilligan, J. 11, 13, 35, 36, 63, 83, 86–7, 97
Gill, P. 95, 106, 107, 109–12
Girard, R. 39–40, 42
Glasser, M. 83, 90
globalization 32–3, 40, 43, 74, 77
'good/bad split' 28
Good Friday Agreement 21, 101
group-actor terrorist 95

group analysis 8–13
group identity 112
group process and globalization 32–3

hallucinatory fusion 78
Hamas 31, 32, 42, 110
harassment and stalking 84–5
Harbidge, P. R. 121–2
Hare, R. 106
Harris, Eric (Columbine Massacre) 82–9
HCR-20 116
Heidegger, Martin 37–8
Henry VIII of England 24
Hezbollah 31, 42, 107
Holder, Eric 107
Hole, G. 74
Hopper, E. 10–11, 13, 14, 97
Horgan, J. 99, 108
humanity 30, 32, 36, 43
Hume, John 27
humiliation 41; and disrespect 35; and injustice 29–32, 33
Husserl, Edmund 37–8
hypocrisy 33, 40

identity 3, 9, 12; group 112; large-group 9, 14, 38, 41–4, 97; male adolescence and 77–9
identity fusion 36
illegal weapons, decommissioning of 45
Imams 123, 124
impotence and inadequacy 68
Independent Press Standards Organisation 121
inequality and post-colonial poverty 28
inequality in power 129
'infantile omnipotence' 67
inflammatory projective identification: ancient regime 52–3; socio-economics 54–6; terrorist 58–9; trans-generational trauma 53–4; unfairness 59–60; western colonialism 56–8
infusion of emotion 42
injustice, humiliation and 29–32
International Centre for the Study of Radicalisation 49
Iraq 6, 7, 11, 21, 56, 58, 100, 130
Irish Peace Process 20–2, 45
Irish Republican Army (IRA) 21, 25, 26, 49
Irish terrorism 23–7
Irrera, D. 101
ISIS 1, 6, 32, 102, 121, 122
Islam and West 33
Islamic fundamentalism 57, 58, 77
Islamic State (IS) 32, 77, 78, 99, 129, 130
Islamic teachings and guidance 123
Islamist terrorism 30–1, 98
Islamophobia 8, 12, 114
Israel/Palestine 30

Jackson, Hughlings 37
Jackson, James 59
Jacques, K. 110
Jihadi ideology 94, 99, 100
jihadist 21, 32, 42, 49–50, 56, 57, 77, 83, 107
Jones, E. 2, 5, 51, 67, 73, 75, 76, 79

Kepel, G. 71, 74–7
Kernberg, O. 62, 102
Kernberg, O. F. 106
King, M. 96
Klein, M. 62
Kleinot, P. 1, 2, 4–5, 8
Klein, Sydney 64
Kleobold, Dylan (Columbine Massacre) 83–9
Knights Templar 102
Kobrin, N. 100, 102
Kohut, H. 8, 83, 88, 106
Kundera, M. 64
Kurdistan 110

language of relationships 22
Lapshyn, Pavlo 2, 131
large-group identity 9, 14, 38, 41–4, 97, 112
Lebiger-Vogel, J. 72, 77
legitimate targets for killings 26
Leuzinger-Bohleber, M. 72, 77
Liberation Tigers of Tamil Eelam (LTTE) 110
Lloyd, Monica 4–5
London 1, 2, 5, 6, 26, 49, 50, 84, 85, 92, 94, 123, 129, 131
London Bridge attack 2, 131
lone-actor terrorist 109, 110, 112, 113
lone attackers 49–50
Luke (Columbine Massacre) 82–92

McGuinness, Martin 49, 57, 58
McVeigh, Timothy 88
Mahler, M. S. 88
Mair, Thomas 2, 131
male adolescence and identity crisis 77–9
male adolescent development 72
Mandela, Nelson 7, 57, 58
Manne, A. 102

Maoist strategy 30
Martin, Abby 56
Mashal, Khaled 32
Mason, O. 110
Mason, O. K. 95
massification, aggregation and 10–11
media, role of 16
medium secure unit (MSU) 82–4
Meloy, R. 8, 14, 62–4, 96, 99–100, 113
mental disorder and terrorism 95, 107; diagnosis 110–11; evaluation 107–8; lone-actor terrorist 109; psychiatrist 114–16; psychoanalytic approach 106, 111–13; psychopathy 106; suicide bomber 109–10; trajectory 108–9
mental illness 4, 5, 27, 37, 38, 105, 130–1, 134, 135
Merari, A. 110
Middle East 2, 6, 7, 21, 28, 29, 31, 51, 55, 56, 58, 78, 99, 109, 110, 134
Miller, L. 95, 98
'Mirroring and Attunement: Self Realization in Psychoanalysis and Art' (Wright) 87
Mitchell, George 45
modernity and secularism 71
Morgan, David 3
mortality rate 76
Motz, A. 14
Muir, J. 122
Multi-level Guidelines for the Assessment and Management of Group-Based Violence 116
muslim community 5, 100, 114; and mental health services 121–2; faith community 122–3; recovery approach 123–5
myths and Judaeo-Christian religion 40

narcissism 78, 83, 86–8, 90, 95, 96, 98, 100, 102, 106, 108, 113
National Health Service (NHS) 114
neo-Jacksonian approach 37–8
Nepal 30
9/11 attacks 2, 6, 12, 16, 20, 27, 40, 56, 58, 70, 105, 128, 130
Nitsun, M. 9–10, 13, 14
noble cause, terrorist 99–101
Northern Ireland 20–2, 26, 29, 30, 31, 38–9, 44, 45, 56, 98, 101, 135; Catholic grievances 28; against English hegemony 24–5; power of tactics 25
Northern Irish Catholics 25
North London riot 129–30
Norway 102, 108

OBJECT-feeling 67
object-seeking antisocial tendency 15
'Oedipus Rex' 86
Oklahoma bombings (McVeigh) 88
Omer, Mulla 41
'one man's freedom fighter is another's terrorist' 7

Pakistani community 5, 99, 132, 133
Palestine Liberation Organization (PLO) 32, 59
Palestinians 29, 30, 32, 55, 79, 100, 107, 110–12
Papousek, H. 68
Papousek, M. 68
parades 38–9
Paris shooting 101
pathological narcissism 88, 102, 106, 113
'pawn in the game' 49
Peace Process 26, 45
personality disorder 96
Peru 29, 30
Phillips, Trevor 121
pilgrimage to hajj 124
Pine, F. 88
Pious Passion: The Emergence of Modern Fundamentalism in the United States and Iran (Riesebrodt) 71–2
PIRA *see* Provisional Irish Republican Army (PIRA)
political context 97–8
political roots of Irish terrorism 23–7
political terrorism 30, 97–8
political violence 22–3, 96
population-level intervention 132
post-9/11 action 40, 58
Post, J. M. 111
post-traumatic stress 128–9
poverty 3, 7, 16, 28, 54, 57–8, 74, 75, 78
Pratt, D. 72–3
predatory aggression 62
Presbyterianism 24
Prevent strategy 5, 113–15, 121
projective identification 48–9; *see also* inflammatory projective identification
promises, fundamentalism 74
Provisional Irish Republican Army (PIRA) 23, 25–7, 30
psychiatrist 4, 95, 105, 108; confidentiality and disclosure 115; in counter-terrorism 114–15; psychoanalytical 27, 98; risk assessment tools 116; stigma 116
psychoanalysis 2, 8–13, 15, 16, 54, 68, 87, 96–7

psychoanalytic approach 106; communication violence 111; group identity 112; risk assessment 112–13; transgenerational trauma 111–12
psychoanalytic contribution 112–13
The Psychopathic Mind: Origin, Dynamics, Treatment (Meloy) 66
psychopathology 61, 83, 84, 89, 95–6, 99, 103, 106–8, 110
psychopathy 3, 63, 95, 106, 107
psychosis 3, 12, 36, 38, 39, 43, 52, 83, 89, 107, 108, 130
psychotic illness 3, 51–2, 83, 107, 108, 113
psychotic process 35–7, 107–8
public health approach 132–4
public health problem 131
purification practice 41–2
push-pull factor 90–1, 99, 100

Qur'an 122, 124, 125

radicalisation 1–5, 7–8, 20, 49, 128; mental illness and terrorism 130–1; public health approach 132–4; risk of 92
Radicalisation Awareness Network 134
rage 3, 8, 10, 11, 14–16, 54, 55, 58, 59, 62–4, 66, 73, 78, 83, 86, 88, 100, 106, 113
rational actors 25
rational argument 28
realpolitik 29
Reddy, V. 67
reform of policing 45
regression 37–9, 43
religion and nationalism 53
religious fundamentalism 44, 49–52, 57, 71, 74–9
religious-political programme 31
reparative process 37–8
The Revenge of God. The Resurgence of Islam, Christianity, and Judaism in the Modern World (Kepel) 71
Riesebrodt, M. 71–2, 76–7
Rigby, Lee 2
Roberts, K. 99
robust security response 26
Rohr, Elisabeth 3
Roman Catholic nationalist community 30
Roof, Dylan 59
Royal College of Psychiatrists 115, 116, 131
Royal Ulster Constabulary 26

Sacco, F. C. 9
sacred values 24
sadomasochistic quality 53
Safeguarding children and Young people: roles and competences for health care staff 114
Sageman, M. 31
Sandler, J. 9
Sartre, J. P. 7
Saudi Arabia 7, 57, 109
Scotland 24
self aggression 63–4
Sendero Luminosa (Shining Path, Maoist) 29
sense of agency 67–8
sense of efficacy 67
September 11 attacks 19
7/7 bombing 2, 6, 94, 131
Shiite Muslim 33
Simon, J. D. 109
Singapore 109
Social Darwinism 52
Social Democratic and Labour Party 27
social system 44
socio-economics 54–6
Somali community 122, 124
South Africa 7, 31, 44–5, 55, 57, 58
stalking and harassment 84–5
stigma 116
Stout, C. 15
suicide 132
suicide bomber 2, 4, 13, 54, 79, 84, 94, 95, 109–11, 131
Suit, Maktuno 4
Summers, A. 73
Sun newspaper 121
Sunni Muslim 33
sustainable economic development 45
Syria 58, 77–8, 102, 109, 130

Taliban 4, 7, 41, 84
Taylor, P. J. 110
Taylor, Richard 4–5
terror 7, 12, 14, 25, 26, 37, 58, 70–3, 75, 76, 78, 79, 94, 100, 130
'Terror, fundamentalism and male adolescence' (Rohr) 3
terrorism 6–7, 25, 97; analysts of 31; and fundamentalism 1–3, 11, 14, 43, 55, 70–4; Irish 23–7; pathways 4; political 97–8; prevention 129; psychoanalysis 96–7; psychoanalysis and group analysis 8–13; psychopathology 95–6; radicalisation 130–1; risk assessment 112–13; role of media 16; with violence 55
Terrorism and War: Unconscious Dynamics of Political Violence 8

terrorist 58–9, 98–9; activity 22–3; attack 97; criminal background 101; *vs.* freedom fighter 7–8; noble cause 99–101; pathological narcissism 102; trajectory 108–9; violence 35
terrorist-prone individual 9
Terrorist Radicalization Assessment Protocol-18 (TRAP-18) 113, 116
Thought paralysis: tolerance, and the fear of Islam (Dalal) 12–13
threat *vs.* 'predatory aggression' 62
Tomkins, S. 67
trans-generational trauma 53–4, 111–12
trauma 23, 42, 97; psychological 128–9; transgenerational 53–4, 111–12; and uncertainty 44; and violence 8–11, 13, 14, 96
The Tree of Life/ Faith in Recovery approach 123–5
Trevmow, S. W. 9
Trump, Donald 33, 51, 52, 89
Tuman, B. 101

Ulster Defence Association (UDA) 25–6
Ulster Scots Presbyterians 24
Ulster Volunteer Force (UVF) 25–6
unconscious, aggression 64
unfairness 29, 59–60
'unfortunate collateral damage of war' 36
United Kingdom 24
utility and cost/benefit analysis 36

Vernon, M. 53–4, 56
Vietnam Nam 57
violence: and aggression 63–6, 65–6; communication 111; deficit and neglect 66–8; disturbance and deviance 62–3; disturbance/disorder 63–5; Irish Peace Process 20–2; psychotic aspects of 51–2; terrorist activity 22–3; trauma and 8–11, 13, 14, 96
violent crimes 35–6
Violent Extremist Risk Assessment (VERA) 116
violent jihadists, fundamentalists and 42
Volkan, V. 40–2, 97
Volkan, V. D. 9, 13, 14
vulnerability 1, 4, 11, 19, 89, 103, 134
Vulnerability Assessment Framework 114

'war on terror' 6, 8, 12, 20, 27–8
'war on terror generation' 8
Welldon, E. V. 14, 15, 35
'Welshness' 51
Welsh terrorist 50
western colonialism 56–8
Winnicott, D. W. 14, 15, 67
Wolf, E. S. 88
World Trade Center bombing 75
Wright, K. 87

Yakeley, J. 4–5, 8, 14, 96, 99–100, 113

Zionist encroachment 55

Printed in Great Britain
by Amazon

65005170R00093